WINDJAMMER COOKING

SKETCHES AND TEXT

BY

DEE CARSTARPHEN

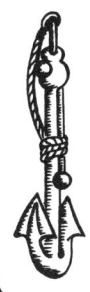

© 1989 DEE CARSTARPHEN
ALL RIGHTS RESERVED
ORIGINALLY PUBLISHED AS "WINDJAMMER WORLD"
BY DOWN EAST BOOKS
© 1979 BY THE AUTHOR
SECOND PRINTING 1982

LIBRARY OF CONGRESS CATALOG CARD NUMBER: 89-91049
ISBN 0-9607544-3-1

PUBLISHED BY PEN AND INK PRESS
P.O. BOX 235, WICOMICO CHURCH, VA. 22579

PRINTED IN THE U.S.A.

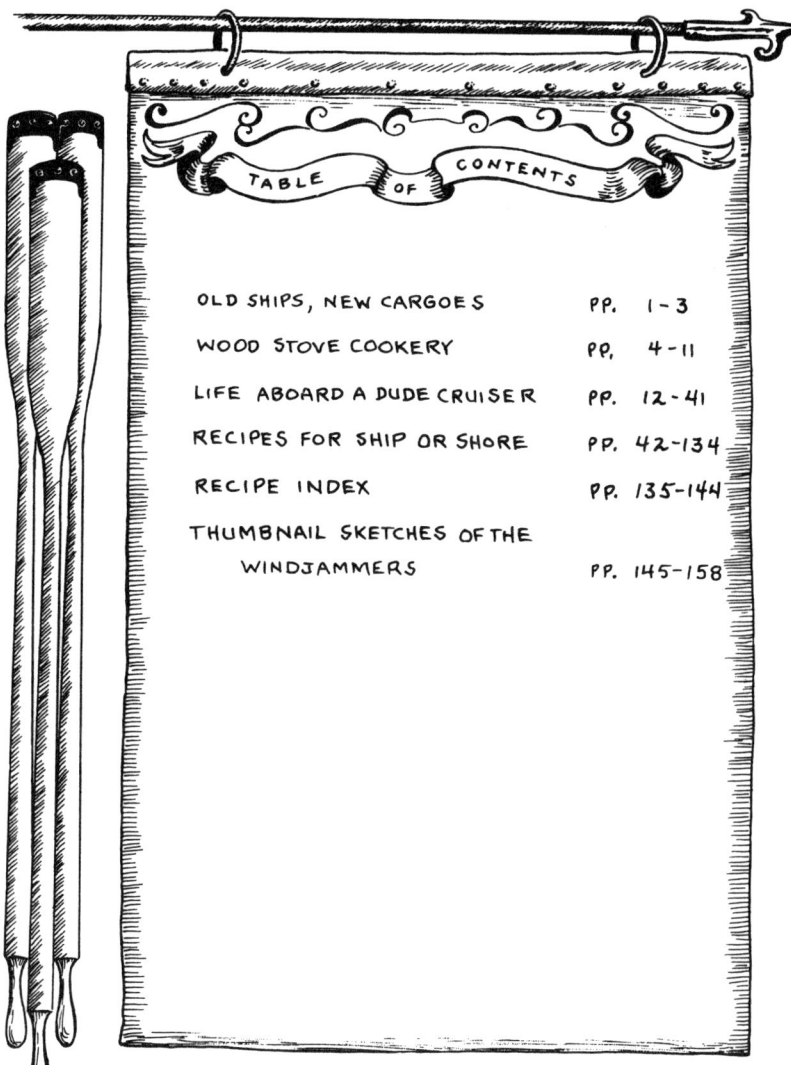

Table of Contents

OLD SHIPS, NEW CARGOES	pp. 1-3
WOOD STOVE COOKERY	pp. 4-11
LIFE ABOARD A DUDE CRUISER	pp. 12-41
RECIPES FOR SHIP OR SHORE	pp. 42-134
RECIPE INDEX	pp. 135-144
THUMBNAIL SKETCHES OF THE WINDJAMMERS	pp. 145-158

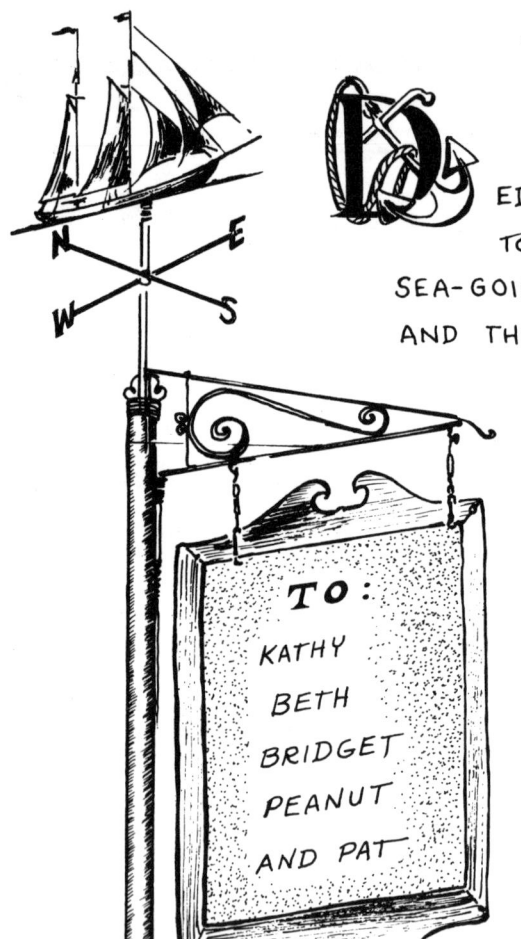

EDICATED TO ALL THOSE SEA-GOING COOKS AND THEIR HELPERS WHO HAVE WORKED SO HARD TO BE PART OF THE SAILING SHIP AND HER MYSTIQUE.

TO:
KATHY
BETH
BRIDGET
PEANUT
AND PAT

WINDJAMMER COOKING   By Dee Carstarphen

Along the northeastern coast of the United States, from Nantucket to Penobscot Bay, more than a dozen windjammers* ply their trade during the summer months. Some of these ships are pure sailing vessels with no inboard engines. Wind and tide set the schedule for their cruises.

Most of these windjammers hail from Maine. Camden, Rockland and Rockport are their traditional home ports. The picturesque harbors sprout masts and rigging that rise above the rooftops, flags and

---

* Although "windjammer" describes any sailing vessel, in New England the word is virtually synonymous with the fleet that carries passengers on sailing vacations.

PENNANTS STREAMING IN THE BREEZE — A HINT OF HOW IT LOOKED ALL THOSE YEARS AGO WHEN SHIPS CARRIED CARGO INSTEAD OF VACATIONERS ALONG THE COAST.

From the mid-1800's until World War 1, coasting schooners carried goods from one port to another.

Often grubby and rough, they worked hard at hauling lumber, lime, granite, fish, salt, ice and other supplies. Later many of their rigs were cut down and pilot houses and engines installed. As truck and rail transport became more economical, the ships were one by one laid up and forgotten in side creeks and by-ways.

Although some have been especially built for this

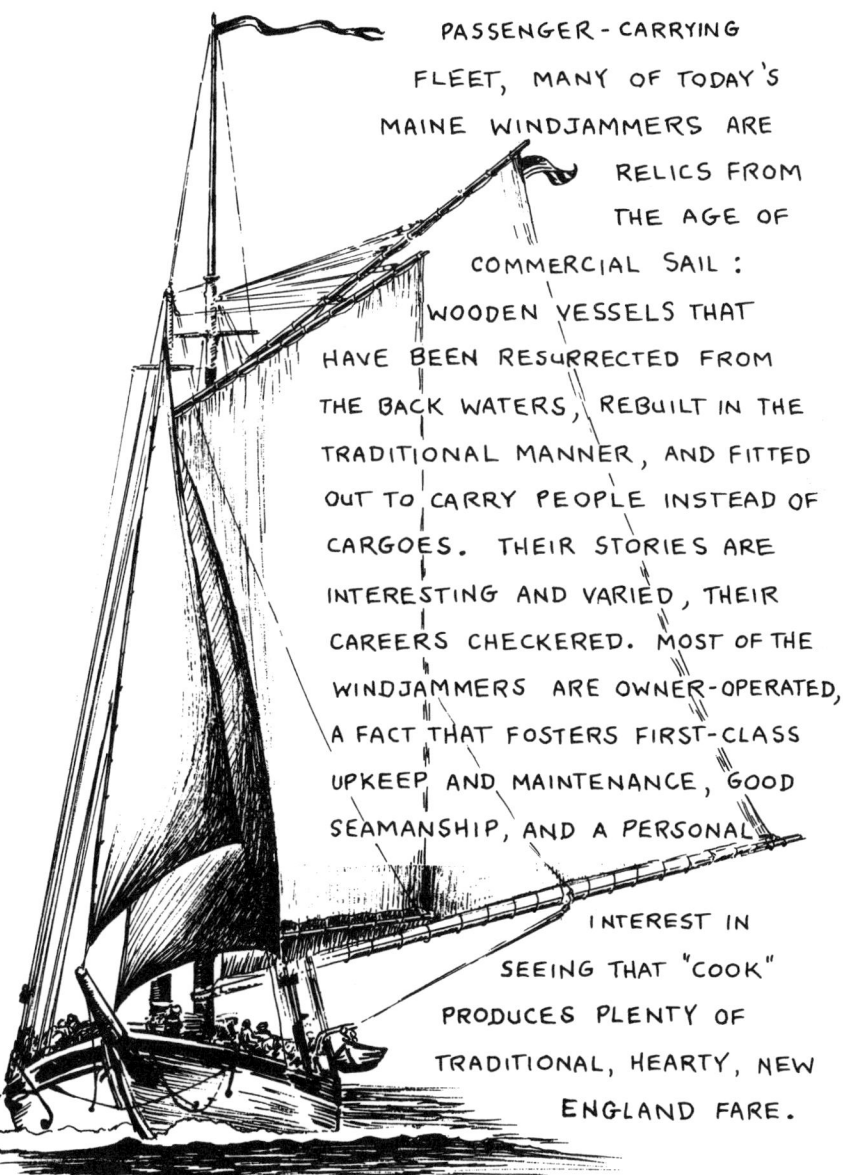

PASSENGER-CARRYING FLEET, MANY OF TODAY'S MAINE WINDJAMMERS ARE RELICS FROM THE AGE OF COMMERCIAL SAIL: WOODEN VESSELS THAT HAVE BEEN RESURRECTED FROM THE BACK WATERS, REBUILT IN THE TRADITIONAL MANNER, AND FITTED OUT TO CARRY PEOPLE INSTEAD OF CARGOES. THEIR STORIES ARE INTERESTING AND VARIED, THEIR CAREERS CHECKERED. MOST OF THE WINDJAMMERS ARE OWNER-OPERATED, A FACT THAT FOSTERS FIRST-CLASS UPKEEP AND MAINTENANCE, GOOD SEAMANSHIP, AND A PERSONAL INTEREST IN SEEING THAT "COOK" PRODUCES PLENTY OF TRADITIONAL, HEARTY, NEW ENGLAND FARE.

MORE OFTEN THAN NOT, A BIG CAST-IRON COOKSTOVE, PERHAPS THE SAME ONE THAT FED THE CREW WHEN THE VESSEL WAS IN THE COASTING OR FISHING TRADE, IS THE HEART OF THE GALLEY. A MIGHTY GOOD THING, TOO, BECAUSE WINDJAMMER CRUISES BREED HUNGER! IT'S HARD TO IMAGINE CIRCUMSTANCES MORE CALCULATED TO WHET WHOLESOME APPETITES: THE SEA IN ALL IT'S MOODS; THE DELIGHTFUL VARIETY OF NEW ENGLAND WEATHER, CLEAR AND CRISP, FOGGY, BREEZY, OR CALM; WHIFFS OF WOOD SMOKE AND

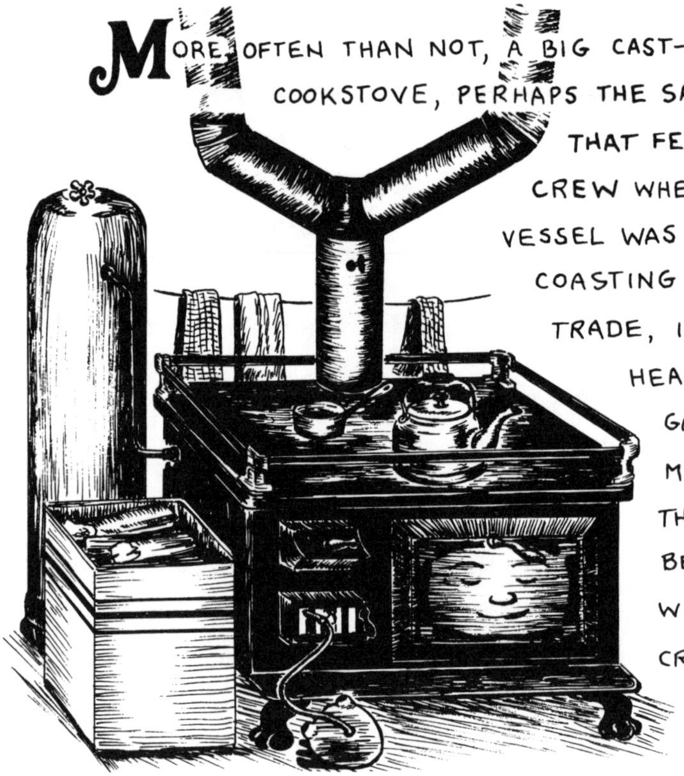

STOCKHOLM TAR, SALT AIR AND FIR TREES, BAKING BREAD; THE SHARED WORK OF HOISTING ANCHOR AND SAILS, THE ADVENTURE OF SHORE PARTIES — ALL SET AGAINST A BACKDROP OF GRANITE-BASED COAST AND ISLANDS MANTLED WITH DARK PINE.

ABOARD THE 120-FOOT SCHOONER "ADVENTURE" (IN WHICH THE AUTHOR WAS COOK FOR TWO SEASONS), THE GALLEY IS DOMINATED BY A BLACK MONSTER OF A STOVE CALLED "MAME". LIKE HER SISTERS ON THE OTHER WINDJAMMERS, "MAME" HAS A DEFINITE PERSONALITY. TYPICALLY FEMALE, SOMETIMES SHE'S OBSTREPEROUS, CANTANKEROUS AND OBSTINATE — SOMETIMES WARM, WILLING AND ANXIOUS TO PLEASE. IT'S ALMOST AS IF SHE HAS OCCASIONAL INDIGESTION ("MAME" LIKES SOME KINDS OF WOOD BETTER THAN OTHERS).

THERE'S NOTHING MORE FRUSTRATING THAN A TON OF METAL THAT HAS TO BE GOTTEN HOT ENOUGH TO FEED

FORTY-FIVE RAVENOUS PEOPLE, AND ONLY GREEN WOOD IN THE BIN TO BURN!

BEING AN OLD BABE (YOU REALLY CAN'T CALL HER A LADY, SHE'S WORKED SO HARD ALL HER LIFE), THE WEATHER BOTHERS HER SOME — THE DAMPNESS PARTICULARLY, MAKING HER SMOKE AND CHOKE AND SPUTTER. THEN SHE NEEDS EXTRA AIR — SUPPLIED BY A BELLOWS CALLED "JEREMIAH", WHO SQUATS UNDER THE STOVE LIKE A BLUE BULLFROG. SOME FOGGY MORNINGS THE RHYTHM OF PUMPING "JEREMIAH" IS THE TEMPO TO SING TO, WHILE "MAME'S" BREATH WHEEZES IN AND OUT, AND THE FLAMES GASP FOR AIR. THEN INDEED, "COOKIE" IS A VERITABLE ONE-ARMED PAPER HANGER — STOKING, PUMPING, MIXING, COOKING, AND KIBITZING ALL AT THE SAME TIME.

BEFORE EACH CRUISE DOZENS OF CRATES FULL OF (HOPEFULLY) DRY WOOD ARE LOADED INTO THE BILGE AREA BEHIND THE MIDSHIPS COMPANIONWAY LADDER. FROM THERE THE WOOD IS CARRIED THREE TIMES A DAY TO FILL THE BOX CLOSE TO "MAME'S" SIDE. IF A FEW BIRCH PIECES ARE LEFT ON TOP IN THE EVENING, THE FIVE A.M. "BRAVE RISER" WILL HAVE THOSE GOOD STARTERS TO USE WITH THE KINDLING. (SOME COOKS RISE A LITTLE LATER AND USE KEROSENE FOR A QUICK HOT FIRE, BUT IT'S NOT THE SAME! BIRCH, ASH, OAK, FIR - - - A PITY TO GIVE UP THOSE FRAGRANCES ON THE EARLY MORNING AIR FOR THAT OF KEROSENE.) AND ONE OF THE BENEFITS OF BEING "FIRE-STARTER" IS THE FEEL AND SMELL OF DAWN OUT AT ANCHOR IN THE ISLANDS - AND THE RARE MOMENT OF BEING ALONE ON DECK.

"**M**AME'S" BROAD, SMOOTH TOP OFFERS EVERY TEMPERATURE FROM FRY TO SIMMER - A TERRIFIC ADVANTAGE, BUT THE COOK MUST MAP THEM. HER OVEN WILL PRODUCE THE CRUNCHIEST BREAD AND PIE CRUSTS EVER TASTED - THE TENDEREST MUFFINS AND CAKES - THE MOST SUCCULENT MEATS.

THE HEAVY IRON WORKS LIKE A CAST-IRON SKILLET OR DUTCH OVEN. DRAFTS AND VENTS NEED ATTENTION. LEAVE 'EM OPEN UNTIL SHE'S ROARING - SHOVE IN THE LEVER LETTING THE HOT AIR CIRCULATE AROUND THE OVEN AND NOT UP THE PIPE. CLOSE DOWN THE DRAFT SO YOU WON'T BE SMOKED OUT. CLOSE IT ALL DOWN TO A SLOW-BURNING GLOW. IN OTHER WORDS, BANK IT, AND GO AHEAD AND BAKE! BUT DON'T THINK TO SLIDE A CAKE IN THE OVEN, DUST THE HANDS AND THAT'S THAT - WRONG AGAIN! THE HOTTEST SPOT IS NEXT TO THE FIRE BOX ON THE TOP SHELF. WHEN THAT CAKE BROWNS, IT MUST BE TURNED, THEN MOVED AWAY FROM THE HOT SPOT AND FINISHED UP ON THE LOWER SHELF TO BROWN THE BOTTOM. NO HEAT INDICATOR OR TIMER CAN HELP YOU HERE. THE TEMPERATURE IS FELT BY HAND

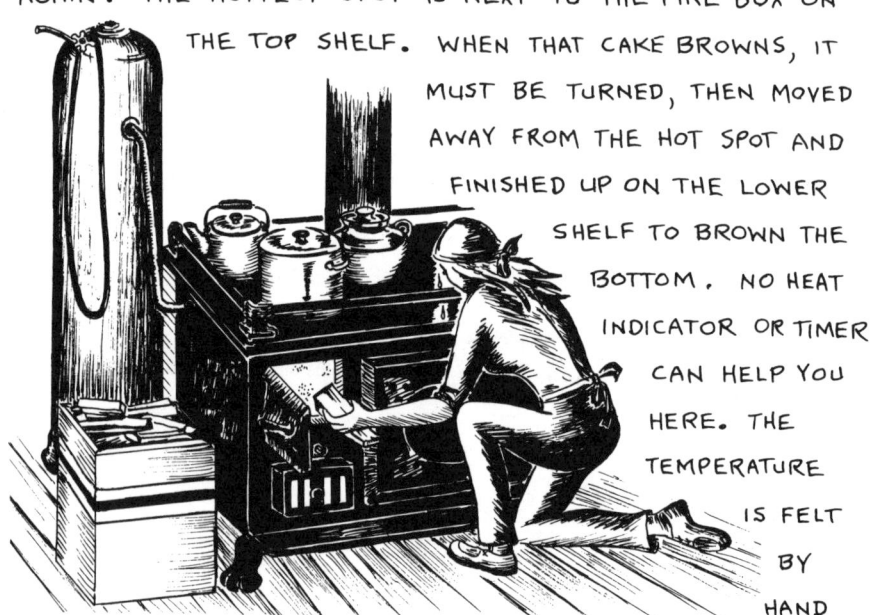

AND A GUT SENSE DEVELOPED ABOUT IT.

All this varies with dry weather or fog – windy or not – sailing or anchored – heeled over or level. "MAME" is a good friend, but if the cook's preoccupied, she might play tricks. Halfway through the week she won't draw, won't get really hot, smokes like a harlot and seems particularly cranky (making cook the same) – she might have an indisposition and need cleaning out. Ashes do pile up! Afterwards she purrs and settles right down. It's a challenge! Perhaps that's why there's a satisfaction never felt with an electric or gas stove – those cold and pristine white enamel machines designed by technicians who have forgotten that warmth is important to the human heart. Enamel does clean easily, but how sweet it is to rub stove black into the old girl and polish her up to a satiny, warm, silvery tone.

THE RACKS OVER "MAME" ARE A PERFECT PLACE FOR BREAD AND ROLLS TO RISE.... TO WARM PLATTERS AND SERVING DISHES AND TO KEEP ALL KINDS OF THINGS HOT WHEN MEALTIME IS NEAR AND THE TOP OF THE STOVE IS OVERFLOWING. LINES ARE SLUNG BEHIND "MAME" FOR DRYING DISH TOWELS (AND SOCKS). ....WET SHOES GO UNDERNEATH. SEA RAILS RUN AROUND THE EDGE OF THE RANGE TOP. THEY CORRAL THE POTS, WHICH HAVE A TENDENCY TO SLIDE ABOUT WHEN THE WEATHER IS LIVELY. KETTLES ARE KEPT FULL AND HOT FOR COFFEE, TEA OR COCOA.

Between meals people can help themselves. If it's cool out, "Mame" is especially popular. So is "Heathcliff". He's "Mame's" constant buddy and is always by her side. He's a bright red water tank piped into "Mame's" fire box. When she's hot, she warms "Heathcliff's" water. A long hose carries hot water from "Heathcliff" to the sinks for washing up the multitude of dishes and pots and pans. Simple, and so important to galley life. "Heathcliff" is gravity-fed from a "day" tank on deck, as are the galley sinks.... a good way to keep track of amounts used.

SUNDAY IS "IN PORT" DAY. PASSENGERS COME ABOARD THAT AFTERNOON, TO BE READY TO SAIL MONDAY MORNING. THEY'RE TOLD SOME OF THE BASIC FACTS IMPORTANT TO WINDJAMMER LIFE, AND SHOWN THROUGH THE SHIP FROM STEM TO STERN (EXCEPT FOR THE ACCOMMODATION FARTHEST FORWARD, WHERE TWO OF THE GALLEY CREW BUNK. IT'S A SMALL CUDDY LIKE A SHOE BOX. THE GIRLS WHO OCCUPY IT HAVE QUITE AN EXERCISE THROUGH THE SUMMER IN GETTING ALONG).

THE MESS ROOM IS TOWARD THE BOW. VISABLE UNDER THE STEPS OF THE MESS-ROOM COMPANIONWAY ARE THE ORIGINAL TREADS, NEARLY WORN THROUGH BY THE TRAMPING BOOTS OF THE SEVENTEEN MEN WHO SLEPT AND ATE HERE WHEN THE "ADVENTURE" FISHED ON THE GRAND BANKS.

THE MESS ROOM HAS FOUR LONG TABLES AND THERE'S SPACE FOR EVERYONE TO EAT TOGETHER AT ONE SITTING. THE BULKHEADS ARE MELLOW, RUBBED WOOD, AND BRASS KEROSENE LANTERNS HANG FROM THE BEAMS. THE GALLEY IS NEXT WITH "MAME" RULING SUPREME. ABOVE THE MAPLE CHOPPING BLOCK, THIRTY DOZEN EGGS ARE STACKED. IT'S A LITTLE SHOCKING TO KNOW THAT THEY'RE THE SUPPLY FOR JUST FIVE DAYS! FOLKS MAY COME FOR DRINKING WATER TO THE OLD-FASHIONED BRASS COUNTRY-STYLE PUMP.

"To pump is to flush,
It makes the waters rush
You've gotta get up early
To avoid the morning crush!"

The toilets (or "heads") are in the passageway and everyone is given a complete demonstration – which levers to push and pull and how many times to pump, etc. Proper operation is important as the heads are mounted below the waterline and if a valve is left open and the head floods – why it could get sloppy! Some ships have installed house-type heads on deck.... a break with tradition, but much simpler. Many head jokes develop

"Hey, Al – I think we have a problem."

Through the summer and the mates become proficient at fixing minor breakdowns. Wash basins (filled from oak barrels on deck), drinking glasses, soap,

TOWELS AND BEDDING ARE SUPPLIED IN THE CABINS. THERE'S AN ELECTRIC LIGHT OVER EACH BUNK FOR READING. AN EXPLANATION IS GIVEN ABOUT USING LIGHTS AND WATER WITH CARE. SAILING SHIPS MUST CONSERVE BOTH. CABIN ACCOMMODATIONS FILL THE CENTER PART OF THE SHIP (THE OLD FISH HOLD) AND CABINS SLEEP TWO TO FOUR. ON "ADVENTURE" THERE'S AN AFTER CABIN WITH A SMALL WOOD STOVE. THE REST OF THE CREW AND THE CAPTAIN HAVE THEIR BUNKS IN THIS AREA....

LIKE PULLMANS BEHIND THE SETEES. THESE ARE SHIPPY, HOMEY BUNKS WITH CURTAINS TO PULL FOR PRIVACY.

TRADITIONALLY, WINDJAMMERS HAVE STURDY DIESEL-DRIVEN YAWL BOATS, HUNG FROM DAVITS ON THE STERN WHEN NOT IN USE. POWERFUL AND EFFICIENT, THEY'RE USED FOR MANEUVERING IN HARBOR OR TO PUSH OR PULL THE MOTHER SHIP IN CALMS. THESE PERKY-LOOKING WORK CRAFT HAVE TOUSLED FENDERS ON THE BOW FOR PROTECTION.

BESIDES HER YAWL BOAT, "ADVENTURE" CARRIES ON HER SIDE DECK THE "SPASTIC SPIDER". THIS IS A SEINE BOAT WITH BANKS OF OARS AND SO NAMED BECAUSE OF THE WAY SHE LOOKS WITH SEVERAL NOVICE ROWERS FLAILING AWAY. THE "SPASTIC SPIDER" IS UTILIZED EVENINGS FOR JAUNTS ASHORE.

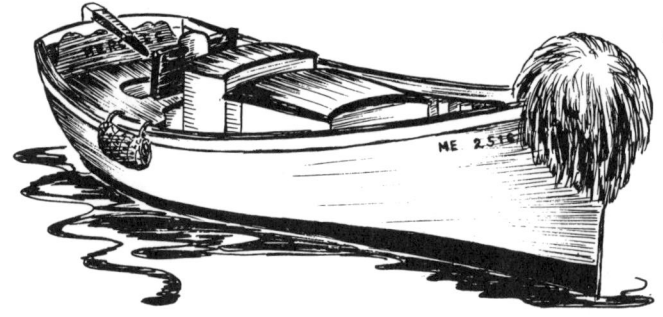

MEALS ARE ANNOUNCED BY RINGING THE SHIP'S BELL AND THE FIRST MEAL SERVED WILL BE MONDAY BREAKFAST. THIS MORNING IS HECTIC. AT FIVE-THIRTY "MAME" IS FIRED UP. THE ASSISTANT COOK AND MESS GIRL ARE BOTH UP WHEN THE SUPPLIES COME AT SIX. THE MATES ARE ON HAND ALSO TO HELP BRING STORES ON BOARD. FRESH FRUITS AND VEGETABLES ARRIVE, AS WELL AS THE FRESH FISH, MEAT AND EGGS. IN BETWEEN STOWING GROCERIES, BREAKFAST MUST BE PUT TOGETHER AND SERVED, AND PREPARATIONS MADE FOR LUNCH. PANCAKES ARE ON THE MENU THIS MORNING, WITH FRESH MAINE BLUEBERRIES ADDED TO THE BATTER. THREE PANS OF SAUSAGE ARE POPPED INTO THE OVEN. THEY MUST BE SHIFTED AROUND TO BROWN. WHEN THE SAUSAGE IS READY AND MOVED TO THE

"HERE'S THE FISH!"

WARMING RACKS, BROWNIES OR BAR COOKIES ARE PUT IN TO BAKE (FOR LUNCH). BISCUITS OR CORNBREAD ARE MIXED AND READY TO FOLLOW (ALSO FOR LUNCH). EXTRA BISCUITS ARE BAKED TO SAVE FOR THE STRAWBERRY SHORTCAKE WHICH WILL BE DESSERT FOR DINNER. THE BIG GRIDDLE SLIDES INTO PLACE OVER THE HOTTEST PART OF "MAME" AND PILES OF HOTCAKES ARE BAKED.

AT THE SAME TIME, THE GALLEY GIRLS ARE STOWING AWAY THE FRESH PRODUCE IN THE BILGE AREA IN THE MESS ROOM. IT STAYS COOL THERE— THE SAME TEMPERATURE AS THE CHILLY SEA.

I'M SURE WE STOWED SOME SPINACH IN HERE SOMEWHERE!

THE ICE COMES DOWN INTO THE MIDDLE OF EVERYTHING — 500 LB. — AND THE BIG ICE CHEST MUST BE LOADED AFTER THAT, PREFERABLY IN THE ORDER THE FOOD WILL BE NEEDED DURING THE WEEK.

THE IRREPLACEABLE GROCER COMES DOWN TO SEE IF EVERYTHING IS O.K. AND IF ANYTHING ELSE IS NEEDED. HE PICKS UP THE LIST OF SUPPLIES FOR NEXT WEEK. PASSENGERS ARE PEERING DOWN THE HATCH, MAKING REMARKS, OFFERING HELP AND

GENERALLY ADDING TO THE CONFUSION. THEY DON'T KNOW QUITE WHAT TO EXPECT YET.

THE NEIGHBORING SHIP'S BELL RINGS, AND FOLKS START TO FILE IN, THINKING IT'S OURS. "YE GODS"! SAYS THE MESS GIRL. THE SYRUP HAS TO BE HEATED AND THE TABLES SET, THEN ALL IS READY. THIRTY-SEVEN HUNGRY, ENTHUSIASTIC AND CURIOUS PASSENGERS POUR IN TO FIND SEATS. THE GIRLS SAVE THE NEAR TABLE FOR THE CREW, WHO ARE ALWAYS A BIT LATE — AND THE SHOW IS ON THE ROAD!

THE CAPTAIN GIVES A SPEECH AS BREAKFAST ENDS. HE TELLS TIME OF DEPARTURE, WHICH DEPENDS ON THE TIDE FOR "ADVENTURE" AS SHE'S A DEEP-DRAFT VESSEL — ALMOST THIRTEEN FEET BELOW THE WATER. PASSENGERS ARE REQUIRED TO WEAR DECK SHOES WHILE

ON BOARD, FOR SAFE FOOTING. THE COOK ASSURES PEOPLE THAT THEY'RE WELCOME IN THE GALLEY AT ANY TIME. THERE ARE ENOUGH PANCAKES FOR A FEW LOCAL FRIENDS WHO DROP BY FOR A BITE, AND ANYONE WHO HAS AN ERRAND TO RUN UP TOWN HAD BETTER DO IT NOW!

DOING DISHES ON A WINDJAMMER IS FUN!

HELP IS ENLISTED FOR DISHES DUTY. POTATOES AND ONIONS ARE PEELED AND SALT PORK IS STARTED IN THE HUGE SOUP POT FOR THE BEST FISH CHOWDER IN THE WORLD!

THE BIG MOMENT ARRIVES! ---

FORWARD LINES ARE CAST OFF, THE YAWL BOAT ("HERCULES") ROARS AND PULLS THE BOW AROUND. ONE STERN LINE IS LEFT BELAYED ASHORE UNTIL THE SHIP IS HEADED IN THE RIGHT DIRECTION. THE PATH OF WATER WIDENS BETWEEN THE SCHOONER AND THE WHARF. SOON THERE'S ENOUGH MOMENTUM AND THE BOW IS THREADING THROUGH THE MYRIAD OF SMALL CRAFT MOORED IN THE BAY.

"HERCULES" LEAVES THE BOW AND MOVES TO THE STERN TO PUSH, CHAFING GEAR TIGHT AGAINST THE TRANSOM. *t*HE GALLEY CREW TRIES TO BE ON DECK TO WATCH THE LEAVE-TAKING. WHEN OUTSIDE CAMDEN HARBOR, THE CRY COMES, "ALL HANDS ON DECK TO RAISE THE MAIN", AND THE PATTERN IS ESTABLISHED FOR THE WEEK. THE MATES EXPLAIN THE "PEAK" AND "THROAT" HALYARDS. ALMOST EVERYONE LENDS A HAND. (THE THROAT'S HEAVIEST, BUT THE PEAK TAKES LONGER!) AFTER THE HUGE MAIN IS SET, THE FORE IS RAISED. THEN UP GOES THE JUMBO AND LAST OF ALL, THE JIB. AND, OF COURSE, "HERCULES" HAS TO BE HAULED UP IN THE STERN DAVITS. THE SCHOONER PAYS OFF, GATHERS HEADWAY AND - "WE'RE SAILING"!

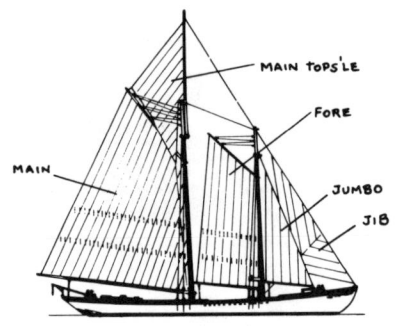

deadeyes and lanyards

IT'S ALSO TIME FOR LUNCH.
MONDAY LUNCH IS ALWAYS FISH CHOWDER— HADDOCK, IF IT'S AVAILABLE. WHAT GOES WITH? WHY, OYSTER AND PILOT CRACKERS, HOT BISCUITS (IN WOODEN BOWLS WITH RED KERCHIEFS FOLDED OVER), CELERY AND CARROT STICKS HEAPED UP WITH BLACK OLIVES FOR CONTRAST, ALWAYS THE PEANUT BUTTER TUB AND JELLY, A RACK OF MUGS FOR COFFEE, PITCHERS OF FRUIT DRINK AND ICED TEA, A HUGE BOWL OF FRESH FRUIT, APPLES, ORANGES, PEACHES, PLUMS, GRAPES, CHERRIES AND BANANAS, AND DON'T FORGET THOSE BROWNIES. ALL THIS MAGNIFICENCE IS SET OUT BELOW, BUT LUNCH IS SERVED ON DECK—WEATHER PERMITTING. A LINE OF PASSENGERS IS FORMED

FROM THE COMPANIONWAY TO THE CABIN, AND ALL THE FOOD IS PASSED ALONG AND READY TO SERVE IN A FEW MINUTES. A BUCKET OF SOAPY WATER AND A HAND MOP ARE PLACED BY THE BREAK IN THE DECK WITH DISH RACKS AND A GARBAGE PAIL, SO PASSENGERS CAN WET-MOP THEIR PLATES AND MUGS AND STACK THEM. THIS MAKES THE CLEANUP JOB BELOW FAR EASIER. THERE'S  TIME ON DECK AFTER LUNCH FOR VISITING, RELAXING OR SAILING. THERE'S SO MUCH SPACE TOPSIDES, SHE SEEMS A MILE LONG — THERE'S NEVER A CROWDED FEELING.

Galley crew may climb aloft and that's the place to get completely away. Three-thirty is witching hour when the girls get together for preparation of the evening meal. Monday night is either roast turkey or chicken, stuffing, corn on the cob, maybe cranberries, peas and mushrooms, salad and strawberry shortcake (fresh berries and real whipping cream). The vegetables vary depending on what's in season that week. The type of stuffing and the way to prepare the bird depend on whim. Ingenuity becomes important. Passengers wouldn't know the difference, but it's deadly dull for the crew to have exactly the same fare every week all summer. It gets to be a game to have variety and interest, and always with a view to eye appeal and nutritional balance. The cook sprouts mung beans, alfalfa seeds and wheat berries — uses wheat germ and whole-grain flours for her breads. She makes her own granola and yogurt. If one of the galley crew wants to try something new, go to it!

There are, each trip, some passengers who are heroes to the cook  and her helpers.... People who show up all the time to help wash and dry the volumes of dishes necessary to feed so many. And there's plenty else to do! After every meal, the wood box by the stove is restacked and the floor swept or swabbed before the mess girl is finished.

There's a good-natured feeling among the windjammers. Any night an anchorage might be shared with another ship. There may be some visiting back and forth or a communal song

fest. Then there's the chance to row the "Spastic Spider" ashore and explore a rural village or the countryside (or offshore lobster town). Maybe some beachcombing,

AND A CHANCE TO WALK OFF THE EFFECTS OF DINNER. MOST EVENINGS HAVE A MUSICAL ENDING IN THE AFTER CABIN – SHARED SEA CHANTYS OR FOLK SONGS IN THE GLOW OF KEROSENE LAMPS OR FIRELIGHT. AND FORWARD IN THE MESS ROOM, THE CLEARED TABLES ARE NOW USED FOR PLAYING CARDS, WRITING UP THE DAY'S ADVENTURES OR POST CARDS TO MAIL AT THE NEXT STOP. OR, HOW ABOUT A SNACK OF LEFT-OVER SHORTCAKE OR A BISCUIT? TO BE CLOSER TO THE ELEMENTS, SOME TAKE SLEEPING BAGS ON DECK AT NIGHT. OTHERS ENJOY THE SNUG FEELING OF THEIR BUNK BELOW.

Early MORNINGS ARE SPECIAL. IT'S SO QUIET ON BOARD. IT'S A GOOD TIME FOR THE COOK TO PLAN HER MENUS FOR THE DAY, TO SAVOR THE SMOKE RISING FROM THE "CHARLIE NOBLE" (SMOKE STACK TO

LANDLUBBERS) – PEACEFUL HARBOR IMPRESSIONS BEFORE THE BUSTLE OF THE DAY. AS SOON AS THE KETTLES BOIL, THERE'S ALWAYS SOMEONE WHO IS READY FOR COFFEE (BESIDES COOK). THEN PUT THE BACON ON – FRY SEVEN LBS. MIX UP MUFFINS AND BREAK THREE FLATS OF EGGS (NINETY!) INTO THE LARGEST BOWL. SCRAMBLED EGGS ARE THE USUAL, BUT IN A VARIETY OF WAYS. COOK'S ASSISTANT COMES YAWNING IN AT SIX THIRTY AND AT SEVEN THE MESS GIRL APPEARS WITH A CHEERY SMILE TO TAKE THE FIRST COFFEE TRAY UP ON DECK.

BOY! WHAT A GREAT SAIL! TOO BAD WE HAVE TO ANCHOR SOON.

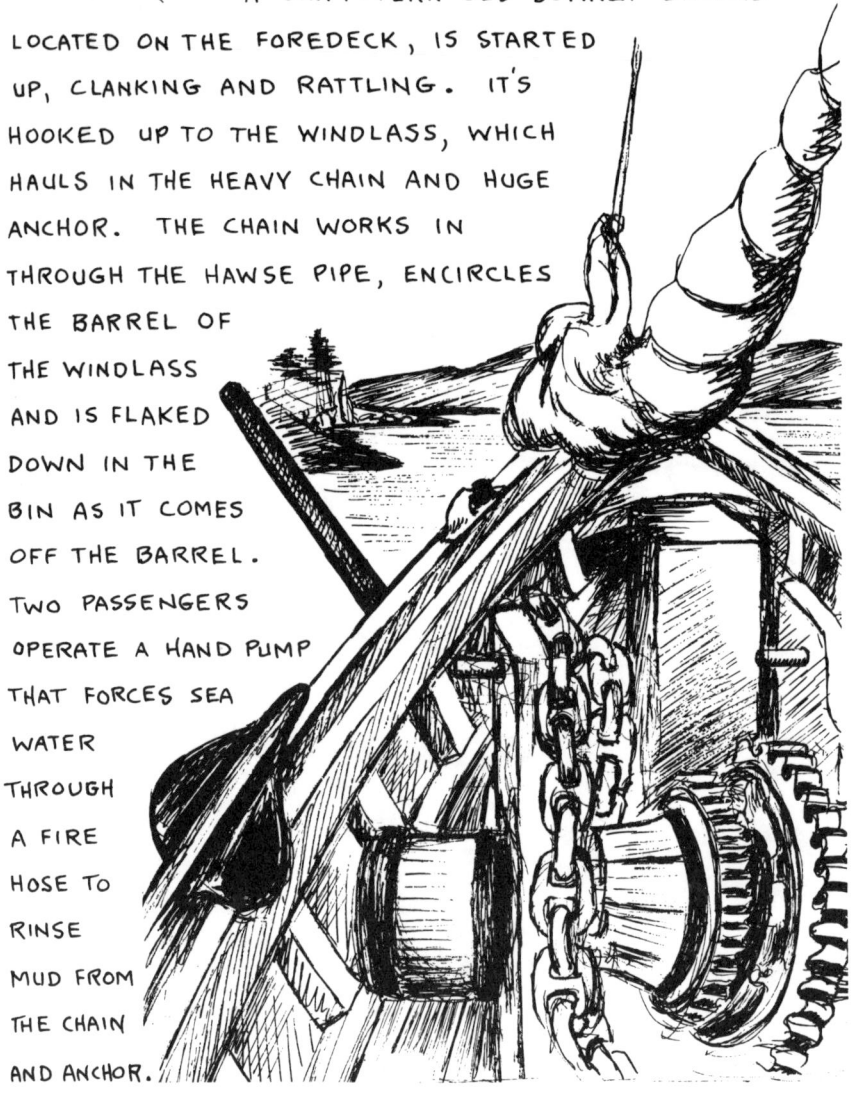

After breakfast, the ship gets under way. The captain sucks on his pipe and takes the wheel. "Big Bertha", a sixty-year-old donkey engine located on the foredeck, is started up, clanking and rattling. It's hooked up to the windlass, which hauls in the heavy chain and huge anchor. The chain works in through the hawse pipe, encircles the barrel of the windlass and is flaked down in the bin as it comes off the barrel. Two passengers operate a hand pump that forces sea water through a fire hose to rinse mud from the chain and anchor.

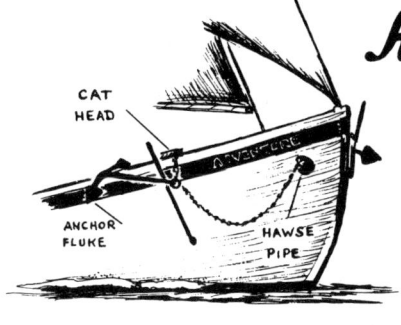

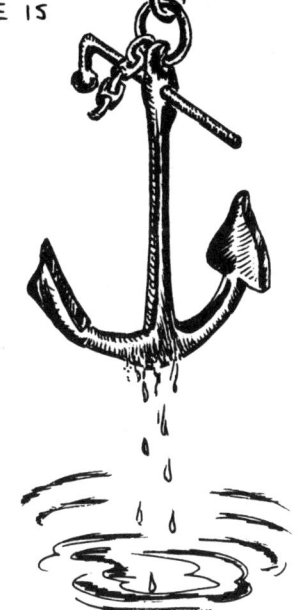

A LONG LINE WITH A HOOK AT THE END IS DROPPED OVER THE BOW AND HOOKED INTO A RING ON THE ANCHOR. WITH A BLOCK AND TACKLE, IT TAKES THREE MEN TO HAUL THE ANCHOR TO THE RAIL. TUCKED INSIDE THE BULWARKS IS A LONG HANDLED WOODEN PADDLE CALLED A "FLUKE SPADE". ONE OF THE MATES INSERTS THIS BETWEEN THE ANCHOR'S FLUKE AND THE SHIP'S HULL TO KEEP THE PAINT FROM BEING GOUGED. THE CHAIN IS SLACKED AS THE ANCHOR IS BROUGHT BACK TO THE CAT HEAD. THE FLUKE IS HAULED UP TO THE RAIL AND LASHED DOWN TIGHTLY TO A CLEAT.

In THE MEANTIME, WITH THE CAPTAIN SHOUTING DIRECTIONS, THE MATES HAVE ORGANIZED THE JOB OF RAISING THE SAILS AND THE SHIP MOVES AWAY FROM THE ANCHORAGE. IF THAT'S NOT POSSIBLE BECAUSE OF WIND, TIDE, OR A TIGHT COVE, THE YAWL BOAT IS PUT TO USE.

"*A*DVENTURE" WILL BE UNDER WAY MOST OF THE DAY. SOME FOLKS TRY TO GET A TAN, BUT A GOOD SHARE

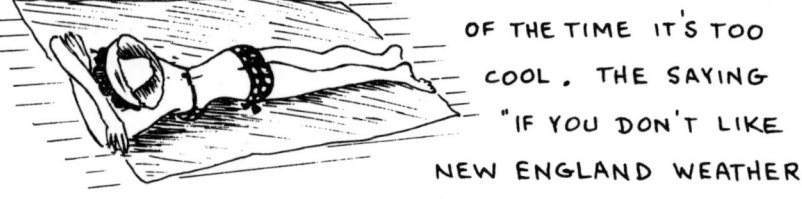

OF THE TIME IT'S TOO COOL. THE SAYING "IF YOU DON'T LIKE NEW ENGLAND WEATHER, WAIT A MINUTE" IS BASED ON FACT. THERE MAY BE HOT SUN, RAIN AND COOL FOG ALL IN ONE DAY — A BATHING SUIT ONE MINUTE, A SWEATER THE NEXT.

Tuesday LUNCH IS A BIG HOT POT OF SOME KIND WITH CRUSTY BREAD, SALAD AND COOKIES. THE GALLEY GIRLS MAY TAKE ON DECK A VARIETY OF FRUITS AND MELONS. PASSENGERS JOIN IN TO CHOP IT ALL UP AND PILE IT IN WATERMELON SHELLS. MIGHTY PRETTY, AND TASTES EVEN BETTER! TUESDAY EVENING DINNER MIGHT BE ROAST LAMB AND PILAF, VEGETABLE, HOMEMADE BREAD, SALAD AND CAKE OR COBBLER. BY NOW FOLKS HAVE STOPPED BEING CONCERNED ABOUT WHETHER OR NOT THERE WILL BE ENOUGH FOOD — THERE ALWAYS IS!

From here on the days mix and blend and flow in a relaxed way. Aft by the wheel, the course is followed on the chart. There may be an impromptu race with another schooner. Porpoise may play under the bow, rolling with the waves. Sea stories abound and the mates go about sailorly chores for the upkeep of the ship.

Passengers may join in with some of these - painting, knotting, splicing, mending canvas, or learning a bit of simple navigation. They might plot the course or take a sight. Whatever the pleasure or whim of the moment - do it! Bed down in a coil of line for a nap, stencil the ship's silhouette on a shirt or jacket, or paint a

WATERCOLOR OF A FOG-SHROUDED ISLAND. SPECIAL THINGS COME ALONG TO MAKE THE TRIP UNFORGETTABLE. LOBSTER BAKE IS ONE! L.B.! ALL WEEK EVERYONE LOOKS FORWARD TO L.B. DAY. GASTRONOMICALLY IT'S A HIGHLIGHT (FOR LOBSTER-LOVERS). PASSENGERS LIKE IT, BOTH FOR THE FOOD AND THE PICNIC AIR OF THE COOKOUT ASHORE. THE GALLEY CREW LOVE IT AS THE WORK IS ALL DONE BEFORE GOING ASHORE.... SORT OF LIKE A NIGHT OFF. THE ONLY ONE WITH MIXED FEELINGS IS THE CAPTAIN WHO HAS THE BURDEN OF PICKING THE RIGHT WEATHER, THE RIGHT DAY, AND THE RIGHT ISLAND. HE TRIES TO FIND A SMALL ISOLATED SPOT NOT ALREADY TAKEN BY ANY OF THE OTHER WINDJAMMERS TRYING TO DO THE SAME THING.

THERE ARE SEVERAL PLACES ALONG THE COAST WHERE LOBSTERS MAY BE PURCHASED EARLY IN THE DAY. THE CRITTERS ARE STASHED ON DECK IN THEIR CRATE, COVERED

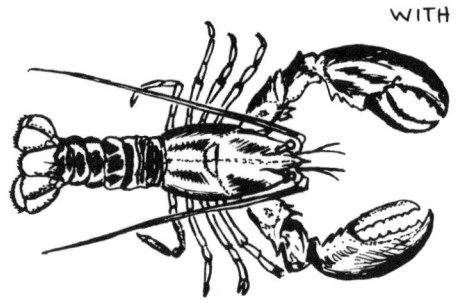

WITH CANVAS, DROOLED AND SQUEALED OVER, AND DOUSED REGULARLY WITH SALT WATER TO KEEP 'EM ALIVE AND KICKING.

There's an air of excitement when the big ship anchors. Everyone gathers gear to take ashore – an extra sweater or windbreak, hiking shoes or boots, bags for beach combing, bug repellant, cameras. The first people in the "Spastic Spider" are those who've opted to help gather wood for the fire. They take the big galvanized tub that serves as cookpot. The second load brings the galley crew and many crates with the picnic goodies.

33

*t*HE GANG ASHORE HAVE SPREAD OUT HUNTING DRIFT-
WOOD FOR THE MATE WHO'S STARTED THE FIRE.
THERE'S A SALTY TANG IN THE AIR. GRANITE ROCKS AND
GRAVEL BEACHES — PINEY WOODS, SEAWEED, WILD ROSES
AND BERRIES — MINGLED ODORS! SNACKS ARE SPREAD
OUT FOR ALL TO MUNCH. BATCHES OF RAW VEGETABLES
AND DIPS — CRACKERS AND CHIPS. THERE'S A LARGE WHEEL
OF WISCONSIN CHEESE ON THE MAPLE BOARD AND A JUG OF
LEMONADE HANDY — PEANUT BUTTER AND JELLY, NATURALLY.
PANS OF BUTTER ARE PUSHED CLOSE TO THE FIRE TO MELT.
THE FIRE ROARS, THE SEA WATER IN THE TUB BOILS AND
THE GUYS HAND IN THE FIRST BATCH OF CRITTERS. THEY'RE
HEAPED OVER WITH SEA WEED — THUS THEY STEAM (15-20
MINUTES) FOR THE BEST FLAVOR IN THE WORLD! THE TUB
IS LIFTED AND DUMPED ONTO A DARK-GREEN BED OF
WEED. BRIGHT RED LOBSTERS, STEAMING AND FRAGRANT!
CAMERAS CLICK — A SIGHT TO INSPIRE AND REMEMBER.

*C*OME AND GET 'EM! THERE'S DRAWN BUTTER AND WHITE WINE, PLUS SALADS AND SNACKS.

SIT ON A ROCK, WATCH THE SUNSET, AND SAVOR THE EXPERIENCE. THE LAST BATCH IS STEAMING AND READY — SECONDS, ANYONE? THE CAPTAIN HOLLERS "THERE'S HOT DOGS HERE FOR THOSE WITH MORE SENSE THAN TO EAT THOSE THINGS!" ONCE IN A WHILE THE TIDE AND BEACH ARE RIGHT FOR CLAMMING AND A LAYER OF CLAMS IS STEAMED IN THE WEED WITH THE LOBSTERS. THEY'RE SWEET AND SUCCULENT

TO CONQUER SIR LOBSTER:

① FIRST TWIST OFF CLAWS
② CRACK CLAWS WITH A ROCK
③ SEPARATE TAIL PIECE — BEND BACK UNTIL IT BREAKS
④ BREAK FLIPPERS OFF TAIL
⑤ PUSH MEAT OUT OF TAIL OR CRACK WITH A ROCK
⑥ BREAK OFF SMALL CLAWS — SUCK MEAT OUT
⑦ UNHINGE BACK
⑧ OPEN BODY — CRACK SIDEWAYS GOOD MEAT INSIDE
⑨ TRY THE "TOMALLEY" OR LIVER — A DELICACY, IT'S GREEN WHEN BOILED

TO SIP RIGHT FROM THE SHELL. TO THE GALLEY, L.B. DAY ALSO MEANS PIE, SO THE HOMEMADE BERRY OR APPLE PIES ARE LAID OUT. BY THE FIRE ARE MARSHMALLOWS, CHOCOLATE BARS AND GRAHAM CRACKERS FOR S'MORES (SHADES OF SCOUTING). CAPTAIN BOILS UP HIS FAMOUS SAILOR'S COFFEE AND STIRS IT WITH A SALTY STICK. STRONGER THAN LOVE AND BLACKER THAN SIN — SOMEHOW JUST RIGHT!

NEW WOOD IS PILED ON THE FIRE; TIME TO SING OR STARE DREAMS INTO THE FLAMES. THERE'S A FEELING OF CONTENTMENT. EVERYONE IS REPLETE; FIRE, WIND AND SUN BURNED AND READY TO ROW HOME TO THE LOVELY SCHOONER SILHOUETTED IN THE DUSK.

DURING THESE FEW DAYS, TIME IS FORGOTTEN AND PEOPLE LIVE FOR THE MOMENT.

THE AMOUNT OF FOOD STEADILY DIMINISHES IN THE ICE-BOX, THE BILGE, AND IN THE LOCKERS. COOK BAKES JUICY, TENDER HAM AND SIMMERS THE BEAN POTS FOR HOURS ON THE BACK OF THE STOVE. THE SMELL OF PIES AND BREAD BAKING PERMEATES THE SHIP AND IT ALL CULMINATES IN FRIDAY NIGHT'S

pièce de résistance — a tremendous roast beef with all the trimmings. Then, evoking memories of grandpa's farm, hot lazy summer days, walking on the railroad tracks, willow whistles, tin dippers of icy water from the well, the best **Homemade Ice Cream** ever tasted!

Here on the schooners, there are the same kind of freezers used on the farm.... old wooden buckets with metal cans and their wooden-bladed dashers. They're pulled out of the bilge on Friday afternoon and the gals run around whipping up enthusiasm for the job — and job it is! Canvas is placed on deck and chunks of ice are wrapped and beaten until crushed. It takes quite a lot for the two eight-quart freezers. After the metal cannisters with the ice-cream mixture are fitted into the buckets, the lids secured and cranks bolted on, crushed ice and rock salt are sprinkled alternately into the space around the cans. Ready! A volunteer

A WEIGHTY AFFAIR!

(PREFERABLY HEAVY) SITS ON A CUSHION ATOP THE MACHINE AND PASSENGERS TAKE TURNS AT CRANKING. SLOW AND STEADY FOR THE LONG HAUL. ADDITIONAL SALT AND ICE ARE ADDED DURING THE PROCESS. WHEN THE HANDLE IS BEASTLY HARD TO TURN, THE CRANKING IS DONE. THE TOPS ARE OPENED AND THE DASHERS REMOVED AND SCRAPED (CARE MUST BE TAKEN NOT TO GET SALT IN THE ICE CREAM). EVERYONE WANTS A TASTE. THE CRANKING TAKES ABOUT THIRTY MINUTES, BUT THE ICE CREAM IS SMOOTHEST IF IT IS ALLOWED TO "RIPEN" AN HOUR OR TWO, SO THE BUCKETS ARE WRAPPED IN THE CANVAS AND LEFT UNTIL AFTER DINNER. WHY IS THIS ICE CREAM EVERY BIT AS GOOD AS GRANDMA'S? IT'S ALL THOSE EGGS, WHOLE MILK AND WHIPPING CREAM. DIATETIC IT AIN'T, BUT IT SURE IS GOOD! ONE CAN OF VANILLA AND ONE SOME OTHER FLAVOR ARE MADE. FLAVORS INCLUDE: FRESH FRUIT OR BERRY, MAPLE NUT, COFFEE, CHOCOLATE, LEMON CREAM, JAMOCCA NUT, OR MINT. AND TO TOP IT OFF, THERE'S A TRAY WITH CHOCOLATE SYRUP, BUTTERSCOTCH SAUCE, BERRIES, NUTS AND CHERRIES. MMMMM!

BY FRIDAY — TOO FULL TO PULL!

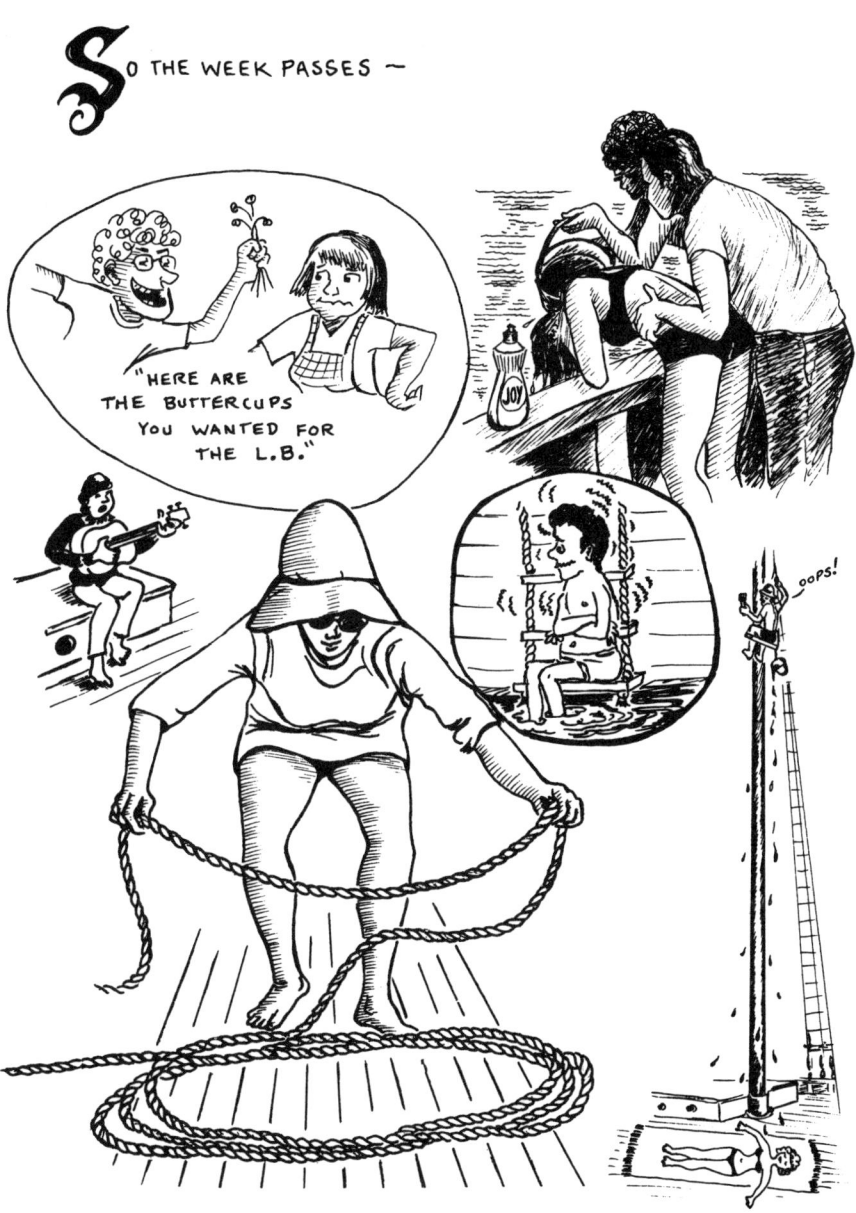

ALMOST BEFORE THE PASSENGERS KNOW IT, THE SCHOONER IS OUTSIDE CAMDEN HARBOR AND IT'S SATURDAY MORNING. THE SAILS ARE FURLED ONE LAST TIME AND THE YAWL BOAT IS PRESSED INTO SERVICE.

THE COOK AND HER HELPERS SAY GOODBYE TO WEEK-OLD FRIENDS AND SPEND THE AFTERNOON SCRUBBING THE GALLEY COMPLETELY AND RESTOCKING STORES TO BE READY TO START THE WHOLE THING OVER AGAIN — USING THOSE GOOD OLD SEA-TESTED, SCHOONER-PROVED WINDJAMMER RECIPES.

APPETIZERS dips snacks

RAW VEGETABLE DIPS

#1
- 1 C MAYONNAISE
- 2 TSP. LEMON JUICE
- ½ C CHOPPED PARSLEY
- 1 TBLSP. GRATED ONION
- 2 TBLSP. CHOPPED CHIVES
- DASH WORCESTERSHIRE
- ½ C WHIPPED CREAM
- ¼ TSP. SALT
- ⅛ TSP. PEPPER
- ¼ TSP. PAPRIKA
- ¼ TSP. CURRY PWD.
- 1 MINCED CLOVE GARLIC

MIX ALL TOGETHER AND CHILL FOR A COUPLE OF HOURS.

#2
- 1 C MAYONNAISE
- 1½ C CHILI SAUCE
- 1 SMALL GRATED ONION
- 2 TSP. HORSERADISH
- 2 TSP. MUSTARD SEED
- TABASCO TO TASTE

MIX ALL TOGETHER AND CHILL UNTIL SERVING TIME. SOUR CREAM MAY BE USED IN PLACE OF THE MAYONNAISE.

↑ ↑ ↑ ↑ ↑ ↑ ↑

SERVE EITHER OF THESE DIPS WITH STRIPS OF RAW CARROT, GREEN PEPPER, CELERY, CAULIFLOWER, ZUCCHINI, TURNIP, CUCUMBER, RADISHES OR MUSHROOMS.

SPINACH DIP
FOR CRACKERS OR CHIPS (RAW VEGETABLES TOO!):
- 1 C CHOPPED, COOKED SPINACH (WELL DRAINED) - RAW SPINACH MAY BE USED
- 1 C MAYONNAISE, CREAM CHEESE, SOUR CREAM OR PLAIN YOGURT
- 1 TSP. SEASON-ALL
- 1 CHOPPED GREEN ONION
- 1 TSP. LEMON JUICE
- 1 TSP. HORSERADISH

MIX ALL TOGETHER. YOU MIGHT WISH TO ADD CRUMBLED BACON OR CHOPPED RED PIMIENTO. TO SERVE, SPRINKLE THE TOP WITH PAPRIKA OR DECORATE WITH STRIPS OF RED PIMIENTO.

SUNSHINE DIP

8 oz. cream cheese　　　½ c mayonnaise
2 tsp. finely chopped onion　2 cloves garlic, pressed
½ c chopped parsley　　dash pepper
2 tsp. anchovy paste　　1 hardboiled egg (put yolk
　　　　　　　　　　　　aside and chop white fine)

Mix all the ingredients together and dress the top with the crumbled or sieved yolk.

RED-HOT DIP

2 c sour cream　　1 envelope Spatini spaghetti sauce mix

Mix together and sprinkle the top with chopped parsley.

SHRIMP DIP

1 8 oz. pkg. cream cheese　　1 can shrimp (drained)
1 can Campbells cr. of shrimp soup　2 tsp. lemon juice
⅛ tsp. garlic pwd.　　　paprika

Mix all together and sprinkle the top with paprika.

HAM DIP OR SPREAD

2 c ground ham or luncheon meat (fine blade)
1 - 8 oz. pkg. cream cheese　　1 tblsp. mustard
1 c mayonnaise or sour cream　　¼ c sweet pickle
1 tblsp. finely chopped onion　　　relish

Mix all together and garnish with chopped parsley.

LOBSTER OR CRAB DIP

1 C CHOPPED LOBSTER OR CRAB MEAT
1 - 8 OZ. PKG. CREAM CHEESE   1 TSP. MUSTARD
1 TSP. SEASON-ALL   1 TBLSP. PWD. SUGAR
1/4 TSP. GARLIC SALT   2 TBLSP. DRY WHITE WINE
1/2 C MAYONNAISE   1 TBLSP. MINCED ONION

MIX ALL TOGETHER. HEAT IN THE TOP OF A DOUBLE BOILER. STIR UNTIL SMOOTH. SERVE HOT OR COLD WITH CRACKERS OR CHIPS.

CLAM POT

MINCE AND SIMMER IN 1/4 C BUTTER:
  1 MEDIUM ONION, CHOPPED   1/2 C CHOPPED GREEN PEPPER
  1 MASHED CLOVE GARLIC   1 TSP. MINCED PARSLEY
ADD: DASH TABASCO
     1 TSP. OREGANO   1 TSP. LEMON JUICE
     DASH CAYENNE   2 C CHOPPED CLAMS, WITH JUICE

SIMMER 5 MINUTES. ADD 1/2 C DRY BREAD CRUMBS. PLACE MIXTURE IN A BUTTERED 9" SQUARE PAN. TOP WITH GRATED SWISS OR AMERICAN CHEESE AND SPRINKLE WITH PARMESAN CHEESE. BAKE AT 350° FOR 30 MINUTES. SERVE HOT OR COLD WITH CRACKERS. - YOU MAY USE 2 CANS OF CHOPPED CLAMS IN PLACE OF THE FRESH.

CLAM DIP

2 C STEAMED, CHOPPED CLAMS   1 - 8 OZ. PKG. CREAM CHEESE
1/2 C MAYONNAISE   1/2 TSP. DRY MUSTARD
1/4 C CHOPPED GREEN PEPPER   2 TSP. LEMON JUICE
1/4 TSP. SALT   DASH PEPPER
2 TSP. CHOPPED CHIVES   DASH TABASCO

DRAIN CLAMS AND SAVE LIQUID TO ADD LATER FOR PROPER DIPPING CONSISTENCY. MIX ALL INGREDIENTS. TOP WITH PAPRIKA OR PARSLEY.

SEVICHE

USE ANY RAW FIRM WHITE FISH, CUT IN ½" PIECES. (ON "ADVENTURE" WE OFTEN USED HADDOCK OR COD) COVER WITH LEMON JUICE AND REFRIGERATE FOR AT LEAST THREE HOURS. (FISH WILL BECOME OPAQUE.) DRAIN THE LEMON JUICE AND ADD (FOR EACH CUP OF FISH) 2 TBLSP. FINELY CHOPPED ONION, 2 TBLSP. FINELY CHOPPED GREEN PEPPER, ¼ C CHOPPED TOMATOES, DASH TABASCO, AND SALT AND PEPPER TO TASTE. CHOPPED PARSLEY, CELERY OR CUCUMBER MAY ALSO BE ADDED IF YOU WISH.

PICKLED FISH

LAYER LEFTOVER COOKED FISH IN AN EARTHENWARE CASSEROLE WITH THINLY SLICED ONIONS (RED ONIONS ARE ESPECIALLY NICE). MIX AND HEAT: ¾ C WINE VINEGAR, ¼ C WATER, 1 TBLSP. OLIVE OIL, JUICE OF 1 LEMON, 1 MINCED CLOVE GARLIC, 1 CRUSHED BAY LEAF, 6 PEPPERCORNS, 1 TSP. SALT, 1 CHOPPED SPRIG OF PARSLEY, AND ¼ TSP. THYME. POUR OVER FISH AND REFRIGERATE.

SNACK NOTES

BREADS

SCHOONER PANCAKES (FOR 4)

Beat two eggs well. Add 2 C sour milk (whole or canned milk may be soured with vinegar or lemon juice). Mix together 2 C flour, 2 tsp. baking pwd., 1 tsp. baking soda, and ¼ tsp. salt. Fold into egg-milk mixture. Add 6 tblsp. melted butter. Beat well and bake on a hot griddle.

BUCKWHEAT CAKES (FOR 6)

Combine 2 C buckwheat flour with 1 C white flour, 3 tblsp. sugar, and 2 tsp. salt. Crumble 1 yeast cake into ½ C warm water. When dissolved, add 2 C warm milk and ¼ C melted butter. Stir liquid into dry mix and beat until smooth. Cover and let rise overnight. In the morning, stir in ½ tsp. soda that's been dissolved in 1 tblsp. water, and one beaten egg. Bake on a hot griddle.

CORN GRIDDLECAKES (FOR 4)

½ C cornmeal	¾ tsp. baking soda
1 ½ C boiling water	⅓ C sugar
1 ¼ C sour milk	1 tsp. salt
2 C flour	1 egg, beaten
1 tsp. baking pwd.	4 tblsp. melted butter

Add cornmeal to boiling water and cook five minutes. Turn into a bowl. Add milk and dry ingredients that have been mixed and sifted. Add egg and butter. Bake on a hot griddle.

OATMEAL PANCAKES (FOR 4)

MIX TOGETHER 1 1/2 C REGULAR ROLLED OATS AND 2 C SOUR MILK. BEAT IN 1 C FLOUR, 1 TBLSP. SUGAR, 1 TSP. BAKING SODA, 1 TSP. SALT AND 2 BEATEN EGGS. ADD 1/4 C MELTED BUTTER. BAKE ON A HOT GRIDDLE.

BISCUITS (MAKES 16)

SIFT: 2 C FLOUR, 3 TSP. BAKING PWD., 1 TSP. SALT.
DROP IN: 6 TBLSP. SHORTENING AND CUT IN WITH A PASTRY BLENDER UNTIL THE DOUGH IS LIKE COARSE MEAL.
MEASURE: 3/4 C MILK. MAKE A WELL IN THE CENTER OF THE FLOUR MIX AND POUR IN 1/2 C MILK. WORK WITH A FORK UNTIL THE DOUGH CLINGS IN A BALL. ADD MORE MILK IF NEEDED. DROP BY TBLSP. ON A BUTTERED COOKIE SHEET, OR TURN OUT ON A FLOURED BOARD AND ROLL OUT 1/2" THICK. CUT ROUNDS WITH A BISCUIT CUTTER. DIP IN BUTTER AND PLACE ON SHE   BAKE AT 425° UNTIL BROWN (12-15 MINUTES).

VARIATIONS: CHEESE - ADD 1/2 C GRATED CHEESE TO THE FLOUR.
ORANGE OR LEMON - ADD 1 TBLSP. GRATED ORANGE OR LEMON RIND.
HERB - ADD 1 TBLSP. MIXED HERBS TO THE FLOUR.
SEED - ADD 1 TBLSP. CARAWAY, SESAME, POPPY OR DILL SEED.
NUT - ADD 1/2 C ANY CHOPPED NUTS.
BUTTERMILK - USE BUTTERMILK INSTEAD OF SWEET MILK AND ADD 2 TSP. BAKING SODA TO FLOUR.
WHEAT OR GRAHAM - SUBSTITUTE 1 C WHEAT OR GRAHAM FLOUR FOR 1 CUP WHITE.

FOR SHORTCAKE DESSERT - CUT IN 2 EXTRA TBLSP. BUTTER AND ADD 1/2 C SUGAR TO THE DRY INGREDIENTS.

MAINE MUFFINS (MAKES ABOUT 10)

- 2 C FLOUR
- 1 TBLSP. BAKING PWD.
- 2 EGGS
- 1 C MILK
- ¼ CUP SUGAR
- ½ TSP. SALT
- ¼ C MELTED BUTTER

SIFT DRY INGREDIENTS. MAKE A WELL IN THE CENTER. BEAT EGGS AND ADD TO BUTTER AND MILK. POUR ALL AT ONCE INTO THE FLOUR WELL. STIR JUST ENOUGH TO MOISTEN. LINE MUFFIN TINS WITH CUP LINERS OR GREASE WELL. FILL CUPS ⅔ FULL. BAKE IN A 425° OVEN ABOUT 25 MINUTES.

VARIATIONS AND ADDITIONS:

- ½ C FINE CUT DATES
- ½ C FINE CUT APRICOTS
- ½ C CHOPPED PEACHES
- ½ C CHOPPED NUTMEATS
- ½ C MASHED BANANA
- ½ C RAISINS OR CURRANTS
- ½ C FINE CUT PRUNES
- ½ C CHOPPED APPLE
- ½ C MASHED PUMPKIN
- SPICES TO DRY INGREDIENTS
- ½ C WELL-DRAINED CRUSHED PINEAPPLE
- 6 SLICES COOKED, CRUMBLED BACON

BLUEBERRY OR CRANBERRY MUFFINS — USE MAINE MUFFIN RECIPE, BUT INCREASE SUGAR TO ⅓ C AND FOLD INTO THE BATTER BEFORE THE DRY INGREDIENTS ARE COMPLETELY MOIST — 1 C FRESH BERRIES (LIGHTLY FLOURED) OR 1 CUP CHOPPED CRANBERRIES (WITH 1 TSP. GRATED ORANGE OR LEMON RIND).

TRY DIPPING THE TOPS OF HOT MUFFINS IN MELTED BUTTER - THEN CINNAMON-SUGAR.

BRAN MUFFINS (MAKES 1 GALLON OF BATTER)

- 2 C - 100% NABISCO BRAN
- 2 C - BOILING WATER — POUR ON BRAN — ALLOW TO COOL.
- 2⅓ C SUGAR
- 1 C OIL
- 4 EGGS

{ CREAM OIL TO SUGAR AND ADD 1 EGG AT A TIME, BEATING AFTER EACH

- 1 QT SOUR MILK — ADD TO CREAMED MIX AND BEAT WELL.

SIFT TOGETHER: 5 C FLOUR, 5 TSP. SODA, 1 1/2 TSP. SALT.
ADD — 4 C KELLOGG'S ALL BRAN
FOLD — INTO MOIST MIXTURE.
ADD — 1 C RAISINS IF DESIRED.
STORE IN A COVERED CONTAINER IN REFRIGERATOR.
USE AS NEEDED. DIP OUT — DO NOT STIR. BAKE AT 375°
20 MINUTES OR UNTIL DONE.

OATMEAL MUFFINS (MAKES 12 MEDIUM)

1 C ROLLED OATS   1 C SOUR MILK
1 C FLOUR   1/2 TSP. SALT
1/2 TSP. BAKING SODA   1 1/2 TSP. BAKING PWD.
1/2 C MELTED BUTTER   1/2 C BROWN SUGAR, PACKED
1 EGG, BEATEN

COMBINE OATS AND SOUR MILK. SOAK 30 MINUTES. SIFT
FLOUR, SODA, SALT AND BAKING PWD. ADD BUTTER, BROWN
SUGAR AND EGG TO OATMEAL MIXTURE. BLEND. STIR IN DRY
INGREDIENTS UNTIL JUST MOISTENED. SPOON INTO GREASED
MUFFIN PANS. BAKE AT 350° — 25 MINUTES.

CORN BREAD

1 C YELLOW CORNMEAL   4 TSP. BAKING PWD.
1 C FLOUR   1 C MILK
1/4 C SUGAR   1 EGG
1 TSP. SALT   1/4 C MELTED BUTTER

COMBINE DRY INGREDIENTS. ADD MILK, EGG AND BUTTER.
POUR INTO A GREASED 8" SQUARE PAN. BAKE AT 425°
25 MINUTES OR UNTIL WELL BROWNED.

CHEDDAR SPOON BREAD

1 CAN CR. CORN (1 LB.)   1½ C GRATED CHEDDAR CHEESE
⅓ C MELTED BUTTER   ¾ C MILK
1 C CORN MEAL   2 EGGS, BEATEN
1 TSP. SALT   ½ TSP. BAKING SODA
1 CAN (4 OZ.) RED PIMIENTOS

MIX ALL INGREDIENTS EXCEPT PIMIENTOS AND CHEESE — WET FIRST, THEN DRY. POUR HALF OF BATTER INTO A 9 x 9" SQUARE BUTTERED PAN. SPREAD WITH CHOPPED PIMIENTOS AND HALF OF CHEESE. COVER WITH THE REMAINING BATTER AND SPRINKLE WITH THE REST OF THE CHEESE. BAKE AT 400° FOR 30-45 MINUTES. COOL 15 MINUTES BEFORE CUTTING.

SCOTCH OATCAKES

1 C FLOUR   1 ¾ C ROLLED OATS
1 TBLSP. SUGAR   ¼ C WHEAT GERM
1 TSP. BAKING PWD.   ½ TSP. SALT
⅓ C BUTTER   ½ C MILK

MIX DRY INGREDIENTS AND BLEND IN MELTED BUTTER. POUR IN MILK AND MIX UNTIL STICKY. DIVIDE DOUGH INTO EIGHT BALLS AND ROLL OUT ONE AT A TIME — VERY THIN. CUT IN WEDGES (AS A PIE) AND BAKE ON GREASED COOKIE SHEETS AT 375° FOR 15-20 MINUTES UNTIL BROWN. THESE KEEP WELL IF COVERED TIGHTLY.

QUICK COFFEECAKE

<u>SIFT</u>: 2 C FLOUR, ¾ C SUGAR, 2 TSP. BAKING PWD., ½ TSP. SALT
<u>CUT IN</u>: ½ C BUTTER   <u>BREAK</u>: 1 EGG INTO A MEASURING CUP AND FILL WITH MILK TO MAKE 1 C. BEAT AND ADD TO DRY INGREDIENTS WITH 1 TSP. VANILLA.
<u>POUR</u> BATTER INTO A GREASED 9 x 13" PAN. COVER WITH STREUSEL OR FRUIT TOPPING. BAKE AT 350° FOR 30-45 MINUTES.

STREUSEL TOPPING: MIX ½ C BROWN SUGAR, ¼ C FLOUR, 2 TSP. CINNAMON, ¼ C MELTED BUTTER. SPRINKLE OVER BATTER BEFORE BAKING (½ C CHOPPED NUTS MAY BE ADDED TOO).

FRUIT TOPPING: COVER BATTER WITH A LAYER OF THIN-SLICED APPLES, PEACHES OR BERRIES. SPRINKLE WITH BROWN SUGAR (NUTS TOO, IF YOU WISH). BEAT 1 EGG WITH ¼ C CREAM AND POUR ON TOP OF FRUIT. BAKE.

BUTTERMILK COFFEECAKE

- 2 ½ C FLOUR
- ½ TSP. CINNAMON
- ¾ C SUGAR
- ½ C NUTMEATS
- 1 TSP. BAKING SODA
- 1 EGG, BEATEN
- ½ TSP. SALT
- 1 C BROWN SUGAR, PACKED
- ¾ C SALAD OIL
- 1 TSP. CINNAMON
- 1 TSP. BAKING PWD.
- 1 C BUTTERMILK

SIFT FLOUR WITH SALT AND ½ TSP. CINNAMON. ADD BROWN SUGAR AND GRANULATED SUGAR AND OIL. BEAT UNTIL BLENDED AND LIGHT. REMOVE ¾ C AND SET ASIDE FOR TOPPING. ADD NUTS AND 1 TSP. CINNAMON TO IT. TO REMAINING MIX ADD SODA, BAKING PWD., EGG AND BUTTERMILK. MIX UNTIL SMOOTH. SPOON INTO A BUTTERED 9 X 13" PAN. SPRINKLE WITH RESERVED TOPPING. BAKE AT 350° FOR 30 MINUTES.

BANANA BRAN BREAD

BEAT: ¼ C SOFT BUTTER WITH ½ C SUGAR.
ADD: 1 EGG, ¼ C MILK AND 1 TSP. VANILLA.
STIR IN: 1 ½ C MASHED BANANA, 1 ¼ C 40% BRAN CEREAL OR RAISIN BRAN AND ½ C CHOPPED NUTS.
SIFT TOGETHER: 1 ½ C FLOUR, 2 TBLSP. BAKING PWD., ½ TSP. BAKING SODA, AND ½ TSP. SALT.

ADD AND STIR ONLY UNTIL COMBINED. PLACE IN A WELL-GREASED 9 X 5 X 3" LOAF PAN AND BAKE AT 350° ABOUT 50 MINUTES. COOL BEFORE SLICING.

MOIST BANANA BREAD

2 LB. RIPE BANANAS	2 C FLOUR
JUICE OF 1 LEMON	3 WHOLE CLOVES, CRUSHED
3/4 LB. BROWN SUGAR	1/2 TSP. PWD. GINGER
3 EGGS, BEATEN	1/2 TSP. CINNAMON
1/2 LB. SOFT BUTTER	1/2 TSP. NUTMEG
2 TSP. BAKING PWD.	1 TSP. VANILLA

BLEND MASHED BANANAS AND LEMON JUICE UNTIL CREAMY. IN A SEPARATE BOWL, CREAM SUGAR, EGGS AND BUTTER. ADD BANANAS AND MIX UNTIL SMOOTH. SIFT TOGETHER DRY INGREDIENTS AND ADD GRADUALLY TO WET. IF BATTER IS TOO STIFF, ADD UP TO 1/4 C MILK. STIR IN VANILLA. POUR INTO A GREASED BREAD PAN AND BAKE AT 350° FOR 50-60 MINUTES OR UNTIL DONE. LET COOL IN PAN 5 MINUTES BEFORE TURNING OUT.

DATE NUT LOAF

POUR: 1 C BOILING WATER (WITH 1 TSP. BAKING SODA MIXED IN) OVER 1 - 8 OZ. PKG. PITTED DATES, CUT UP. COOL. ADD: 2 BEATEN EGGS, 3/4 C SUGAR, 1 TSP. BAKING PWD., 1/2 TSP. SALT, 2 C FLOUR AND 1/2 C CHOPPED NUTS. BAKE IN A 9" GREASED LOAF PAN IN A 350° OVEN FOR 1 HOUR.

ZUCCHINI BREAD

2 C GRATED ZUCCHINI, 3 BEATEN EGGS, 1 C OIL. TO THESE, ADD 2 C SUGAR (OR 1/3 LESS HONEY), 3 C FLOUR, 1 TSP. BAKING SODA, 1 TSP. SALT, 1/4 TSP BAKING PWD., 3 TSP. CINNAMON, 2 TSP. VANILLA, AND 1 C CHOPPED WALNUTS.

GREASE WELL A 9" LOAF PAN AND BAKE 1 HOUR AT 350°.

CRANBERRY NUT BREAD

3 C FLOUR	2/3 C SUGAR
3 TSP. BAKING PWD.	1 EGG
1/2 TSP. BAKING SODA	3/4 C MILK
1 TSP. SALT	1 C CRANBERRY-ORANGE RELISH
1/2 C BUTTER	OR - 1 C GROUND RAW CRANBERRIES
1 C CHOPPED PECANS	

CREAM BUTTER AND SUGAR. ADD BEATEN EGG AND BLEND. ADD SIFTED DRY INGREDIENTS ALTERNATELY WITH MILK. STIR IN RELISH AND NUTS. POUR BATTER INTO A GREASED 9 X 5" LOAF PAN AND BAKE AT 350° ABOUT 1 HOUR OR UNTIL DONE.

WHEAT ORANGE BREAD

1 1/2 C WHOLE WHEAT FLOUR	1/2 TSP. SALT
1 1/2 C WHITE FLOUR	3/4 C ORANGE JUICE
3/4 C SUGAR	1/2 C MILK
2 TBLSP. GRATED ORANGE PEEL	1/2 C OIL 1 EGG
2 TSP. BAKING PWD.	1/2 C CHOPPED NUTS

COMBINE ALL INGREDIENTS. STIR UNTIL THE DRY PARTICLES ARE MOISTENED... ABOUT 75 STROKES. POUR INTO A GREASED 9 X 5" LOAF PAN. SPRINKLE WITH A MIXTURE OF 1 TBLSP. SUGAR AND 1/2 TSP. CINNAMON. BAKE AT 350° ONE HOUR OR UNTIL A TOOTHPICK INSERTED IN THE CENTER COMES OUT CLEAN.

OATMEAL RAISIN BREAD

2 C FLOUR	2 TSP. BAKING PWD.
3/4 TSP. BAKING SODA	1 1/2 TSP. SALT
1 C ROLLED OATS	1 C RAISINS
1/3 C BUTTER	1/3 C BROWN SUGAR
1 EGG, BEATEN	1 1/4 C BUTTERMILK

CREAM BUTTER AND SUGAR. ADD EGG AND BUTTERMILK. ADD MILK ALTERNATELY WITH COMBINED DRY INGREDIENTS. BAKE AT 350° IN A GREASED 9 X 5" LOAF PAN FOR 1 HOUR.

IRISH SODA BREAD

4 C FLOUR	1/8 TSP. CARDAMOM (OR CORIANDER)
1 TSP. SALT	1/4 C BUTTER
3 TSP. BAKING PWD.	1 EGG, BEATEN
1 TSP. BAKING SODA	1 3/4 C SOUR MILK
1/4 C SUGAR	

MIX FLOUR, SALT, BAKING PWD., SODA, SUGAR AND SPICE. CUT IN BUTTER WITH A PASTRY BLENDER UNTIL CRUMBLY. MIX EGG WITH SOUR MILK. ADD TO DRY INGREDIENTS AND STIR UNTIL BLENDED. TURN OUT ON A FLOURED BOARD AND KNEAD TWO OR THREE MINUTES. DIVIDE DOUGH IN HALF AND SHAPE EACH INTO A ROUND LOAF. PLACE IN GREASED PIE OR CAKE PAN. CUT CROSSES IN TOPS OF LOAVES. BAKE AT 375° 35-40 MINUTES.

<u>VARIATION</u>: OMIT CARDAMOM OR CORIANDER AND ADD 2 C CURRANTS OR RAISINS TO THE FLOUR MIX, WITH 1 1/4 TSP. CARAWAY SEED OPTIONAL.

SPICED PUMPKIN BREAD

1 1/2 C SUGAR	1/2 C RAISINS
1/2 C VEGETABLE OIL	1/2 TSP. BAKING SODA
2 EGGS, BEATEN	1/4 TSP. BAKING PWD.
1 C CANNED PUMPKIN	1 TSP. SALT
1 1/4 C FLOUR	1/2 TSP. ea. ALLSPICE, CLOVES
3/4 C WHEAT FLOUR	1/2 TSP. ea. CINNAMON, NUTMEG

MIX SUGAR AND OIL. ADD EGGS, PUMPKIN AND 1/3 C WATER AND MIX WELL. SIFT DRY INGREDIENTS TOGETHER. ADD TO PUMPKIN MIXTURE AND STIR UNTIL JUST MOISTENED. STIR IN RAISINS. POUR INTO A GREASED 9 X 5 X 3" LOAF PAN AND BAKE AT 350° FOR ONE HOUR. — A MOIST BREAD.

ADVENTURE BASIC BREAD (2 loaves)

SCALD: 2 c whole milk. Add 1/4 lb. butter and let it melt. Add 1/2 c sugar. Stir until it's dissolved and cool until lukewarm. Sprinkle in 3 tblsp. dry yeast and let it proof. After it foams up, add 1 tblsp. salt and work in enough flour (approximately 8 c) to form a soft dough. Turn out on a floured board and knead until satiny. Place in an oiled bowl, brush the top with butter, cover and let rise an hour or until double. Knock down and make into rolls or loaves. Place in 2 greased bread pans. Let rise until double and bake at 375° - 1/2 hour or until brown and done.

VARIATIONS: This recipe may be made with various types of flour, but don't use more than half of a whole grain flour like wheat, rye, graham — the other half white. Wheat germ may be added, or seeds and herbs — try a tblsp. of millet.

CINNAMON ROLLS: Use the basic recipe, but cut 4 tblsp. extra butter into 4 c of the flour. Beat 2 eggs and add to liquid after the yeast has proofed. After the first rising, roll out (1/4 at a time) dough 1/2" thick. Brush with melted butter, sprinkle with brown sugar and cinnamon (raisins and nuts if desired). Roll up as for a jelly roll. Cut 3/4" slices and place in buttered pans. Let rise until double and bake at 375° for 15-20 minutes.

BUTTERMILK CHEESE BREAD

1 C BUTTERMILK	1 C WARM WATER
2 TBLSP. SUGAR	1/2 TSP. BAKING SODA
2 1/2 TSP. SALT	6 C FLOUR
1 TBLSP. BUTTER	1 1/2 C (6 OZ.) GRATED
2 PKG. DRY YEAST	AMERICAN CHEESE

SCALD MILK WITH SUGAR, SALT AND BUTTER. COOL. DISSOLVE YEAST IN WARM WATER AND STIR IN COOLED MILK MIXTURE. STIR SODA INTO 2 C FLOUR. ADD THIS TO MILK MIX AND BEAT UNTIL SMOOTH; ADD GRATED CHEESE AND BEAT IN; ADD REST OF FLOUR TO FORM A STIFF DOUGH. TURN OUT ON FLOURED BOARD AND KNEAD UNTIL SATINY. TURN INTO AN OILED BOWL AND LET RISE UNTIL DOUBLE IN BULK. PUNCH DOWN AND SHAPE INTO TWO LOAVES. LET RISE AND BAKE AT 350° — 30 - 45 MINUTES.

CORNMEAL BRAID

2 C MILK	1/4 C WARM WATER	7 C FLOUR
6 TBLSP. SUGAR	1 PKG. DRY YEAST	CORNMEAL (FOR PANS)
1 TBLSP. SALT	2 EGGS, BEATEN	1 EGG, BEATEN
1/2 C BUTTER	1 C CORN MEAL	3 TBLSP. WATER

SCALD MILK AND STIR IN SUGAR, SALT AND BUTTER. COOL. DISSOLVE YEAST IN WARM WATER AND ADD TO MILK. STIR IN EGGS, CORNMEAL AND 3 1/2 C FLOUR; BEAT. ADD REMAINING FLOUR. TURN OUT ON FLOURED BOARD AND KNEAD UNTIL SATINY. PLACE IN OILED BOWL, COVER AND LET RISE UNTIL DOUBLE. PUNCH DOWN AND LET DOUGH REST 10 MINUTES. DIVIDE DOUGH IN HALF AND EACH HALF IN THIRDS. MAKE THE THIRDS INTO 12" STRIPS. BRAID 3 STRIPS AND PLACE IN GREASED, CORNMEAL SPRINKLED BREAD PANS. REPEAT WITH OTHER THREE STRIPS. LET RISE UNTIL DOUBLE AND BAKE AT 350° 25 MINUTES. MIX EGG AND WATER — BRUSH TOPS OF LOAVES AND BAKE TEN MINUTES MORE.

ANADAMA BREAD

SPRINKLE: 1 1/4 C CORNMEAL INTO 4 1/2 C BOILING WATER. COOL TO LUKEWARM.

ADD: 3 TBLSP. YEAST DISSOLVED IN 3/4 C WARM WATER, 1 C MOLASSES, 1 1/2 TBLSP. SALT, 1/3 C OIL OR BUTTER.

ADD: 4 1/2 C WHITE FLOUR, 4 1/2 C WHEAT FLOUR

TURN OUT ON A FLOURED BOARD AND KNEAD, ADDING FLOUR IF NECESSARY, UNTIL SMOOTH AND SATINY. PLACE IN AN OILED BOWL, BUTTER THE TOP OF DOUGH, COVER AND LET RISE UNTIL DOUBLE IN BULK. PUNCH DOWN AND SHAPE INTO LOAVES. PUT INTO GREASED BREAD PANS THAT HAVE BEEN SPRINKLED WITH CORNMEAL. BAKE IN A 375° OVEN 30 MINUTES OR UNTIL DONE. MAKES 3 LOAVES.

ANDREA'S NEWFOUNDLAND BREAD (3 LOAVES)

- 2 PKG. YEAST
- 3 C WARM WATER
- 10 C FLOUR
- 1 1/2 TSP. SALT
- 2 TBLSP. BUTTER
- 1 C MOLASSES

PROOF YEAST IN 1 C WARM FOR TEN MINUTES. SIFT FLOUR, SALT AND CUT IN BUTTER. MAKE A HOLE IN THE FLOUR AND ADD DISSOLVED YEAST, MOLASSES AND 2 C WARM WATER. MIX THOROUGHLY. KNEAD UNTIL SATINY AND LET RISE UNTIL DOUBLE IN BULK. PUNCH DOWN, SHAPE INTO LOAVES AND PLACE IN GREASED BREAD PANS. LET RISE UNTIL DOUBLE AND BAKE AT 375° FOR 40-45 MINUTES. OR MAKE ROLLS AND BAKE AT 400° FOR ABOUT 12 MINUTES.

OATMEAL BREAD

Mix 2 c warm water, ½ c honey and 1 c oatmeal. Stir in 2 pkg. dry yeast and let proof. Stir in 2 beaten eggs and ⅓ c melted butter. Add 1 tblsp. salt. Mix in 7 to 7½ c flour, in 2 additions. Turn out on a floured board and knead until smooth. Place in a greased bowl, oil top, cover and let rise until double in bulk. Punch down and make into rolls or 2 loaves of bread. Place in 2 greased bread pans, let rise and bake at 400° until done.

The following bread has an interesting taste and texture and uses leftover oatmeal if you've cooked too much for breakfast:

COOKED OATMEAL BREAD

- 1½ c cooked oatmeal, warm
- 2 pkg. dry yeast
- ½ c warm water
- 1 tsp. sugar
- 1 c warm milk
- 1 tblsp. salt
- ¼ c dark brown sugar
- 4-5 c flour

Dissolve yeast and sugar in warm water and allow to proof. Add milk, salt, brown sugar and yeast mixture to the oatmeal stir well, then stir in flour, 1 cup at a time. Turn out on a floured board and knead until smooth, adding flour if necessary. Place in a buttered bowl and turn to coat the dough. Cover and let rise until double. Punch down and shape into 2 loaves. Place in buttered 8 x 4 x 2" pans. Let rise until almost double and bake at 375° 45-50 minutes. After removing from pans, the loaves may be returned to the oven for about 5 minutes for a firmer crust.

WHEAT GERM BREAD

2 C MILK	1/3 C MOLASSES	2 PKG. YEAST
1 1/2 C WATER	2 TBLSP. BROWN SUGAR	1/2 C WARM WATER
1 C WHEAT GERM	1 TBLSP. SALT	1 TBLSP. SUGAR
1/3 C BUTTER	3 C WHEAT FLOUR	4 C WHITE FLOUR

SCALD MILK AND WATER. PLACE WHEAT GERM, MOLASSES, SALT, SUGAR AND BUTTER IN A BOWL. POUR IN HOT MILK AND BLEND. ADD WHEAT FLOUR AND BEAT. LET COOL. DISSOLVE YEAST IN 1/2 C WARM WATER, ADD SUGAR AND STIR UNTIL DISSOLVED. ADD TO COOLED MIX. WORK IN WHITE FLOUR UNTIL YOU HAVE A SOFT DOUGH. TURN OUT ON A FLOURED BOARD, LET DOUGH REST TEN MINUTES AND THEN KNEAD UNTIL SMOOTH. PLACE IN A BUTTERED BOWL, OIL TOP, COVER AND LET RISE UNTIL DOUBLE IN BULK. KNOCK DOWN AND DIVIDE INTO 3 LOAVES. PLACE IN BUTTERED BREAD PANS, LET RISE AND BAKE AT 400° FOR TEN MINUTES AND THEN AT 325° FOR 30 MINUTES.

SPROUTED WHEAT BREAD

2 C WHEAT SPROUTS	5 C WHEAT FLOUR
1/4 C WARM WATER	1 TBLSP. SALT
1 TBLSP. HONEY	2 C WARM WATER
1 TBLSP. YEAST	3 TBLSP. OIL
1/2 C PWD. NON-FAT MILK	3 TBLSP. HONEY

SPROUT WHEAT GRAINS UNTIL THE ROOT IS AS LONG AS THE GRAIN (3 DAYS). MIX WATER, HONEY AND YEAST. LET FOAM (10 MINUTES). MIX PWD. MILK WITH FLOUR AND SALT BEFORE ADDING YEAST MIX. COMBINE WATER, OIL AND HONEY WITH SPROUTS AND STIR THE MIX INTO THE FLOUR. BEAT UNTIL THE BATTER IS SMOOTH AND ELASTIC (1 MINUTE). DROP A CUPFULL ONTO A GREASED SHEET AND LET IT SPREAD INTO A FLAT ROUND. BAKE AT 350° FOR 30 MINUTES. OR BAKE IN SMALL, GREASED LOAF PANS. THIS MAKES A HEAVY, MOIST BREAD WITH A WONDERFUL FLAVOR.

PUMPKIN-RAISIN ROLLS

1 1/4 tsp. salt	1/4 c warm water
1/2 c sugar	1 c mashed pumpkin
1/4 c butter	1 c raisins
1 c hot water 1 env. dry yeast	4 1/2 c flour

Place salt, sugar and butter in a bowl. Add hot water and stir. Dissolve yeast in the 1/4 c warm water and combine with the cooled butter mix. Stir in pumpkin and raisins. Add 2 1/2 c flour and beat well. Stir in 2 more cups of flour. Turn out on a floured board and knead until smooth. Place in greased bowl. Oil top of dough, cover and let rise until double. Make into rolls and place in greased pans. Let rise and bake at 375° about 20 minutes. Makes two dozen.

BETH'S OLD WORLD RYE BREAD

2 c rye flour	2 tsp. salt
1/4 c cocoa	2 tblsp. caraway seed
2 pkg. yeast	2 tblsp. butter
1 1/2 c warm water	2 1/2 c white or
1/2 c molasses	wheat flour

Combine rye flour and cocoa (unsweet). Dissolve yeast in 1/2 c warm water. Combine molasses, the remaining water, salt and caraway seed in large bowl. Add rye flour mix, yeast, butter and 1 c white or wheat flour. Beat until smooth. Spread rest of flour on board with dough and knead in enough to make a smooth, elastic dough. Place in an oiled bowl, turn to coat, cover and let rise until double. Shape into a round loaf on a buttered sheet sprinkled with cornmeal. Let rise. Bake at 375° for 35-40 minutes.

NEW ENGLAND RAISIN BREAD

Mix together 1¼ c warm milk, ½ c sugar and crumble in 2 yeast cakes. Stir until dissolved. When yeast foams, add 1 tblsp. salt, 4 beaten eggs, and ½ c melted butter. Stir in 1 box seedless raisins. Mix in 6¼–6¾ c flour. Turn out on a floured board and knead until satiny. Place in an oiled bowl, turn to coat dough, cover and let rise. Punch down and form into 2 loaves. Let rise in 9 x 5" greased loaf pans and bake at 350° for 30-45 minutes.

DATE-NUT YEAST BREAD

1 pkg. yeast	¼ c warm water
1 - ¾ c milk	1 c brown sugar
2 tsp. salt	½ c melted butter
2 eggs, beaten	6 c flour
1 c chopped dates	½ c chopped nuts

Dissolve yeast in water. Scald milk and add brown sugar, salt and butter. Cool. Add yeast and stir in eggs. Mix dates and nuts into flour. Stir milk mix into dry ingredients. Let rest ten minutes, then turn out on a floured board and knead until smooth. Let rise until double in bulk. Knock down, form into two loaves, and bake at 350° in greased bread pans for 30-45 minutes or until done.

STEPHEN TABER STEAMED BROWN BREAD

(Enough batter for three one-lb. coffee cans)

2 c white flour	2 c rolled oats	1 tsp. salt
2 c cornmeal	2 c molasses	¼ box raisins (opt.)

Mix ½ c boiling water with two heaping tsp. baking soda. Add 3½ c water (total amount of liquid is double the measure of any one of the dry ingredients). Mix all together and pour into greased 1-lb. coffee cans. Cover with foil and place on rack in kettle — 1" of water in the kettle. Cover and steam 3 hours. To turn a loaf out of a can while the bread is still warm, remove the bottom lid and use it to push the loaf out the top. Here's a tip for cutting moist, hot brown bread: circle the loaf with a strong thread, cross the ends and pull the thread through the loaf, creating a slice of whatever thickness you wish. A bread knife tears it up.

"ADVENTURE" GRANOLA — The galley crew found making granola a great pleasure. We would toss in whatever we wanted to, using ingredients at hand. It's often a matter of personal preference. For guidelines in amounts of sweet and oil, you may try the following:

4 c rolled oats	1 c sunflower seed	1/3 c salad oil
1 c wheat germ	1 c chopped nuts	1 tsp. vanilla
1 c cornmeal	2 c all bran	1/4 c maple syrup
1/4 c millet	1 tsp. cinnamon	(opt.)
1/2 c sesame seed	1/2 c honey	

Mix honey, oil and vanilla and stir into dry ingredients. By hand is the best way. Coconut may be added or poppy seed. Spread mix in flat pans and bake at 350° about 25 minutes, stirring once in a while. When golden brown, remove from oven and stir in any dried fruits you wish — 1 c chopped dates or 1 c raisins — dried apple, apricots, etc. Cool and store in a tightly covered container.

On "Adventure", cereal morning is satisfying! When the bell rings, a large pot of hot cereal is ready on the stove. It may be oatmeal, cream of wheat or wheatina — perhaps it's a combination of all three, with wheat germ, brown sugar and pwd. milk stirred in. The tables hold packages of dry cereal, bowls of our granola, raisins, brown sugar, fresh berries or bananas, pitchers of milk, and platters of coffeecake or buns hot from the oven... along with slices of honeydew or cantaloupe (or grapefruit halves) .... a great start for a morning in Maine!

BREAD NOTES

EGG DISHES

Cooking for a windjammer mob limits fixing eggs many different ways. The simplest method is to <u>scramble</u>. There are endless variations.

2 eggs per person are stirred up (with 1 tblsp. water or milk per egg). Seasonings are added — salt, pepper, herbs or seeds.

① Chopped <u>onions and green peppers</u> sautéed in butter. Add eggs and cook and stir until set.

② To the above, stir in chopped <u>tomato</u> and sprinkle the top with grated <u>cheddar cheese</u> and/or chopped parsley.

③ <u>Cottage cheese and chives</u> may be stirred into the eggs while cooking.

④ Cream of <u>mushroom soup</u> or cream of <u>celery soup</u> may be added while cooking. Decorate with chopped <u>pimiento</u>, sprinkle with <u>paprika</u>.

⑤ Heavy <u>cream</u> or chunks of <u>cream cheese</u> make the eggs so smooth and sour cream gives a lovely taste.

⑥ If you sprout <u>mung beans</u> or <u>alfalfa seeds</u>, try stir-frying them a couple of minutes with a little grated onion before adding the eggs.

⑦ <u>Sesame</u>, <u>poppy</u>, <u>caraway</u> or <u>dill</u> seed add an interesting flavor to scrambled eggs.

⑧ Don't forget <u>mushrooms</u> — they're good any way! Eggs are such a marvelous carrier and your breakfast may have a "huevos rancheros" touch or come out with a Chinese taste. The only limit is your imagination.

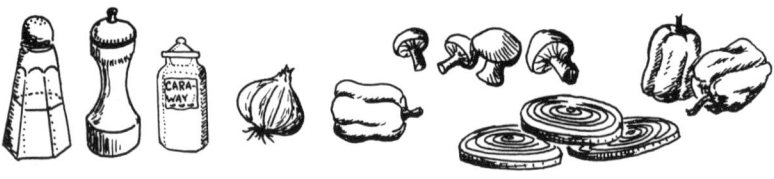

MUSHROOM-EGG POACH (SERVES 6)

SAUTÉ 1 MEDIUM CHOPPED ONION IN 2 TBLSP. BUTTER IN A SKILLET. ADD 1 CAN CREAM OF MUSHROOM SOUP, 1 CAN CHEDDAR CHEESE SOUP, 1 SMALL CAN MUSHROOM PIECES, AND 3/4 SOUP CAN MILK. HEAT ALL TO A BOIL, REMOVE FROM HEAT AND ADD 1/2 C SHERRY. DROP IN 1 OR 2 EGGS PER PERSON. RETURN TO THE FIRE AND SIMMER UNTIL THE EGGS ARE SET. SERVE ON TOAST OR ENGLISH MUFFINS.

RED-EYE POACH (SERVES 6)

SAUTÉ 1 MEDIUM CHOPPED ONION, 1/2 CHOPPED GREEN PEPPER AND 1 MINCED CLOVE GARLIC IN 2 TBLSP. BUTTER IN A SKILLET. ADD 2 CANS (1 LB.) STEWED TOMATOES, 1 TBLSP. WORCESTERSHIRE SAUCE AND 1/2 TSP. BASIL. BRING TO A BOIL, LOWER THE HEAT AND DROP IN 1 OR 2 EGGS PER PERSON. SPRINKLE ON TOP 1/2 C GRATED AMERICAN CHEESE. SIMMER UNTIL EGGS ARE SET. SERVE ON TOAST. A MEXICAN VARIATION IS TO ADD 1 ENVELOPE OF TACO SEASONING MIX TO THE TOMATOES AND SIMMER THIS MIXTURE FOR FIVE MINUTES BEFORE DROPPING IN THE EGGS. — MUY SABROSA!

CREAMED EGGS (SERVES 6)

- 3 TBLSP. BUTTER
- 1 MEDIUM ONION, CHOPPED
- 1/2 GREEN PEPPER, CHOPPED
- 1/4 C FLOUR
- 1 1/2 C MILK
- 1 TBLSP. WORCESTERSHIRE
- 1/2 C GRATED AMERICAN CHEESE
- SALT AND PEPPER TO TASTE
- 1 CAN CREAM OF MUSHROOM SOUP
- PARSLEY
- 6 COARSE-CHOPPED HARD BOILED EGGS

SAUTÉ ONION AND GREEN PEPPER IN BUTTER IN A SAUCEPAN. REMOVE FROM FIRE AND STIR IN FLOUR. GRADUALLY STIR IN MILK. RETURN TO FIRE AND STIR AND COOK UNTIL THICK AND SMOOTH. STIR IN WORCESTERSHIRE, CHEESE, SALT, PEPPER AND MUSHROOM SOUP. IF TOO THICK, THIN WITH MILK. ADD EGGS AND PARSLEY. SERVE ON HOT, SPLIT BISCUITS — OR ON TOAST.

On "Adventure", we sometimes fixed a "Buckeye Brunch" (a name stolen from Schooner "Harvey Gamage"). It's an oven fondue, which is baked for breakfast, but may be laid up the night before.

Buckeye Brunch (serves 6-8)

Butter a rectangular baking pan. Butter ten slices of bread (we like rye) and cut in cubes. Beat 6 eggs well and add 3 c milk, 2 tblsp. parsley, 1 tsp. dry mustard, 1 tsp. salt. Mix bread and egg mixture and add 2 c shredded American cheese. Spread in pan and bake at 350° for an hour or until set.

<u>VARIATIONS</u>: Mix in 1-2 c cooked chopped ham. For lunch, you may add 3 tblsp. fine chopped onion and 1 pkg. chopped frozen spinach. — Grated raw zuchinni is a winner too.

Sausage Buck (serves 6)

- 8 eggs, slightly beaten
- 6 slices bread, cubed
- 1 lb. sausage, cooked and crumbled
- 2 c milk
- 1 c cheddar cheese, grated
- 1 tsp. salt
- 1 tsp. dry mustard
- ½ green pepper, diced
- 1 small onion, diced

Mix all ingredients together and put in a greased 9 x 13" pan. Refrigerate overnight. Bake at 350° for 35 minutes or until firm.

QUICHE

1 - 9" PIE SHELL. PRICK WITH A FORK, BRUSH WITH EGG WHITE (BEATEN TO A FROTH) AND BAKE AT 400° ABOUT SEVEN MINUTES. FOR FILLING: SAUTÉ 1/2 LB. BACON (CUT IN 1" PIECES) UNTIL ALMOST CRISP. DRAIN. SCALD 2 C MILK OR CREAM. COOL A LITTLE AND BEAT WITH 3 EGGS, 1/4 TSP. SALT, DASH PEPPER, DASH CAYENNE, A GRATING OF NUTMEG AND LASTLY, ADD 1 TBLSP. CHOPPED CHIVES. SPRINKLE BACON AND 1 C DICED SWISS CHEESE IN PIE SHELL. POUR CUSTARD OVER. BAKE AT 375° FOR 35-40 MINUTES.

QUICHE WAS USED AS A LUNCHEON DISH AND WITH VARIATIONS:

HAM — SUBSTITUTE CHOPPED HAM FOR THE BACON AND ADD 1/2 TSP. DRY MUSTARD TO THE LIQUID.

VEGETABLE — SAUTÉ IN 1 TBLSP. BUTTER 3/4 C SLICED ONION AND SPREAD ON CHEESE WITH 1/2 SLICED GREEN PEPPER.

OTHER VEGETABLES — SPREAD ON CHEESE 1 C CHOPPED SPINACH, OR GRATED ZUCCHINI, OR MUSHROOMS, OR DRAINED CUT TOMATOES.

SEAFOOD — SPREAD ON CHEESE 1 C CHOPPED LOBSTER, SHRIMP, CLAMS, CHUNKS OF TUNA OR SALMON IN PLACE OF THE BACON.

EGG NOTES

SANDWICHES & STUFFINGS

SANDWICH FILLINGS

CHICKEN OR TURKEY

- 2 C DICED CHICKEN OR TURKEY
- 1 C SLICED CELERY
- 1/4 C FRENCH DRESSING
- SALT AND PEPPER
- 1/4 C TOASTED SLIVERED ALMONDS
- 2 CHOPPED GREEN ONIONS
- 1/2 C MAYONNAISE
- 1/4 C SOUR CREAM

MARINATE MEAT AND CELERY IN FRENCH DRESSING AN HOUR OR SO. SEASON WITH SALT AND PEPPER, GREEN ONIONS AND ALMONDS. DRESS WITH MAYONNAISE MIXED WITH SOUR CREAM. VARY WITH <u>CURRY PWD.</u> OR ADD <u>1 C COOKED RICE</u>. IT'S DELICIOUS IF YOU ADD <u>1 C HALVED SEEDED GRAPES</u>.

EGG SALAD

- 6 HARD BOILED EGGS
- 1/2 C CHOPPED CELERY
- 1 TSP. MUSTARD
- 2 TBLSP. CHOPPED CHIVES
- SALT AND PEPPER TO TASTE
- 1 TSP. CARAWAY OR DILL SEED
- 1/4 TSP. SEASON ALL
- 1/4 TSP. GARLIC PWD.
- MAYONNAISE
- SOUR CREAM

CHOP EGGS FINE AND ADD THE REMAINING INGREDIENTS, USING HALF MAYONNAISE AND HALF SOUR CREAM TO GIVE THE PROPER CONSISTENCY. YOU MAY VARY THIS BY ADDING 1 TSP. CURRY PWD. AND/OR 1/4 C RELISH.

HAM SALAD

GRIND WITH THE FINE BLADE OF A MEAT GRINDER – LEFTOVER HAM AND/OR LUNCHEON MEAT. MIX IN CHOPPED CELERY, MINCED ONION, CHOPPED GREEN PEPPER, WORCESTERSHIRE, MUSTARD AND MAYONNAISE. MEASUREMENTS DEPEND ON YOUR OWN LIKES. OTHER ADDITIONS ARE CHOPPED PICKLES OR CHOPPED PINEAPPLE AND WALNUTS. IF YOU ADD PINEAPPLE, GRATE IN A LITTLE NUTMEG TOO.

TUNA SALAD

- 2 CANS CHUNK TUNA (7 OZ.)
- 1/3 C SWEET CHOPPED PICKLE
- 2 TBLSP. MINCED GREEN PEPPER
- 1 C FINE CHOPPED CELERY
- 2 TBLSP. PARSLEY
- 1/2 C MAYONNAISE
- 1/2 C SOUR CREAM
- 1/2 TSP. SALT & DASH PEPPER
- 2 TBLSP. LEMON JUICE
- DASH CAYENNE

MIX ALL TOGETHER. I LIKE TO ADD 1/2 C CHOPPED APPLE TOO.

SEASONED TOAST

(GREAT TO SERVE WITH SOUP OR AS A CHANGE FROM GARLIC BREAD)
FOR 15 PIECES OF TOAST — MIX:

- 3/4 C SOFTENED BUTTER OR OLEO
- 1 CHOPPED MEDIUM ONION
- 1 TBLSP. CHOPPED PARSLEY
- 2 TSP. SESAME SEED
- 2 TSP. POPPY SEED
- 1/4 TSP. FINES HERBS
- 1/4 TSP. SEASON ALL
- 1 TSP. WORCESTERSHIRE
- DASH PEPPER
- 1/4 C PARMESAN CHEESE

SPREAD ON BREAD, OVERLAP THE SLICES SLIGHTLY ON BAKING SHEETS AND BAKE AT 400° UNTIL TOASTED.

*S*tuffings

STUFFINGS ARE ANOTHER REMINDER OF GRANDMA'S KITCHEN AND FESTIVE HOLIDAY TIMES. IN FACT, MANY PEOPLE NEVER HAVE STUFFING UNLESS IT'S THANKSGIVING OR CHRISTMAS AND THERE'S A TURKEY IN THE OFFING. THERE ARE MANY DIFFERENT WAYS TO FIX A STUFFING AND IT'S A MARVELOUS SIDE DISH WITH ALMOST ANY MEAT OR FISH. IT MAY BE VARIED DEPENDING ON WHAT'S AROUND IN THE LEFTOVER DEPARTMENT.

CORN BREAD STUFFING (10 CUPS)

1 LB. BULK SAUSAGE	1 CHOPPED GREEN PEPPER	1 TSP. SALT
6 C CORNBREAD	1 1/4 C CHICKEN STOCK	1/2 TSP. PEPPER
6 C BREADCRUMBS	1/2 TSP. SAGE	2 LG. ONIONS, CHOP
2 C SLICED CELERY	1/2 TSP. THYME	3 PARSLEY SPRIGS

FRY SAUSAGE AND DRAIN. IN SAUSAGE FAT, SAUTÉ ONIONS UNTIL SOFT. TOAST BREADS AND COMBINE WITH ALL THE INGREDIENTS. IF YOU LIKE, ADD 1/3 C CHOPPED RED PIMIENTO. THIS IS GOOD WITH POULTRY, PORK OR HAM.

TRADITIONAL STUFFING

2 QTS. DRY BREAD, BROKEN UP (ANY KIND OF BREAD WILL DO)

1/2 C WHEAT GERM	1/2 C CHOPPED ONION	1/2 TSP. THYME
1/2 C DICED CELERY	1 TSP. SALT	1/2 TSP. POULTRY SEASONING
2 TBLSP PARSLEY	1/2 TSP. PEPPER	3/4 TO 1 C CHICKEN BROTH
1 LB. BULK SAUSAGE	1/2 TSP. EACH SAGE AND MARJORAM	

FRY SAUSAGE AND DRAIN. IN SAUSAGE FAT, SAUTÉ ONIONS UNTIL SOFT. ADD ONION TO BREAD WITH THE REMAINING INGREDIENTS. YOU MAY ADD 1/2 C CHOPPED NUTS AND/OR 1/2 C RAISINS OR CURRANTS.

RICE STUFFING (5C)

6 SLICES BACON, CHOPPED	1 C CHOPPED CELERY	1/2 C MILK
1/4 C CHOPPED ONION	3/4 TSP. SALT	1/2 C CREAM
4 C COOKED RICE	1/4 TSP. PEPPER	(OR 1 C CHICKEN STOCK)
1 C DRY BREAD CRUMBS	1/8 TSP. SAGE	2 TBLSP. PARSLEY

SAUTÉ BACON WITH ONIONS. POUR OFF ALL BUT 2 TBLSP. GREASE. MIX WITH REMAINING INGREDIENTS. IF YOU LIKE, ADD 1/2 C PINE NUTS.

STUFFING FOR FISH (4 C)

__MIX__ — 5 C DRY BREAD CRUMBS, 1/4 C CHOPPED CHIVES, 1 C CHOPPED CELERY (WITH LEAVES), 1/4 C CHOPPED PARSLEY, 1/2 C CHOPPED WATERCRESS AND 3 BEATEN EGGS.

__SEASON WITH__ — SALT, PAPRIKA, 3/4 TSP. TARRAGON OR DILL SEED, 3 TBLSP. CAPERS AND 1/4 TSP. NUTMEG.

__ADD__ — ENOUGH MILK, MELTED BUTTER OR SOUP STOCK TO MAKE A LOOSE STUFFING.

YOU MAY ADD MORE VEGETABLES TO THIS DRESSING — CHOPPED TOMATOES OR MUSHROOMS, OR GRATED CARROT.

FRUIT STUFFING

SAUTÉ 5 MEDIUM CHOPPED ONIONS AND 5 CHOPPED APPLES WITH 5 SLICES CHOPPED BACON. ADD 1 MINCED CLOVE GARLIC. YOU MAY ADD 1 CAN DICED PEACHES, A SMALL CAN DICED PINEAPPLE AND A FEW CHERRIES. - MANDARIN ORANGES ARE NICE. SPRINKLE WITH THYME, SALT, PEPPER, SAGE AND PARSLEY. ADD RAISINS AND WALNUTS IF YOU WISH. BREAK UP 4 OR 5 SLICES OF BREAD AND MIX IN WITH 2 BEATEN EGGS...AND OH, YES, A LITTLE SWEET BASIL.

PINEAPPLE STUFFING (GREAT WITH HAM OR PORK)

1/4 LB. BUTTER	1/4 C SUGAR
6 SLICES CUBED BREAD	1 LARGE CAN CRUSHED PINEAPPLE
2 EGGS, BEAT SLIGHTLY	OR 2 C CHOPPED FRESH PINEAPPLE

PLACE CUBED BREAD IN A BAKING DISH. POUR MELTED BUTTER OVER THE BREAD. MIX EGGS, SUGAR AND PINEAPPLE AND ADD TO BREAD CUBES. BAKE AT 350° FOR 25-30 MINUTES.

SOUPS

FISH CHOWDER
½ LB. SALT PORK
4 LARGE POTATOES
2 CHOPPED ONIONS
1 CLOVE GARLIC, PEEL AND CRUSH
A FEW CHOPPED CELERY LEAVES
2 C HOT WATER   2 CHICKEN BOUILLON CUBES
1 BAY LEAF   2 TSP. SALT   ¼ TSP. PEPPER
1 TSP. WORCESTERSHIRE   2 LB. HADDOCK FILLETS
2 C CREAM   ½ C DRY WHITE WINE   ¼ C BUTTER   PARSLEY
¼ TSP. DILL WEED OR SEED

FRY UP SALT PORK IN A SOUP POT (OR A FEW SLICES OF CHOPPED BACON). ADD POTATOES, PEELED AND CUBED, ONIONS AND GARLIC. FRY UP FIVE MINUTES OR SO AND COVER WITH HOT WATER. ADD CHICKEN BOUILLON AND CELERY LEAVES. SIMMER UNTIL POTATOES ARE TENDER. THEN ADD BAY, SALT, PEPPER, DILL, WORCESTERSHIRE. BREAK UP FISH, DROP IN AND SIMMER FIVE MINUTES. ADD CREAM, WINE AND BUTTER. GARNISH WITH CHOPPED PARSLEY TO SERVE. FOR A THICKER SOUP, SPRINKLE IN A LITTLE INSTANT MASHED POTATO.   SERVES 8-10

Clam Chowder

SHUCK 1 QT. CLAMS. WASH AND DRAIN MEAT (SAVE LIQUID). CUT HARD PART OF CLAM AWAY FROM THE SOFT. CHOP HARD PART. SAUTÉ A 2" CUBE OF SALT PORK (CUT UP) OR 3 SLICES CHOPPED BACON WITH 1 CHOPPED LARGE ONION AND THE HARD PART OF CLAMS. (5 MINUTES) STIR IN 3 TBLSP. FLOUR AND RESERVED CLAM JUICE. ADD 2 C RAW DICED POTATOES AND HALF A CRUMBLED BAY LEAF. SIMMER UNTIL THE POTATOES ARE TENDER. ADD SOFT PART OF CLAMS, 3 C HOT MILK, AND 3 TBLSP. BUTTER. DON'T BOIL. SEASON TO TASTE.

Lobster Bisque (SERVES 6)

MEAT FROM 2 MEDIUM LOBSTERS. DICE MEAT AND RESERVE. CRUSH SHELLS. ADD TO THEM THE TOUGH END OF CLAWS, 2 1/2 C CHICKEN STOCK AND/OR CLAM JUICE, 1 SLICED ONION, 2 CELERY STALKS AND LEAVES, 1/4 C CHOPPED CARROTS, 2 WHOLE CLOVES, 1 BAY LEAF AND A FEW PEPPERCORNS. SIMMER 1/2 HOUR AND STRAIN. IF THERE'S CORAL ROE, SIEVE IT AND MASH IT WITH 1/4 C BUTTER AND WORK IN 1/4 C FLOUR. POUR 3 C HEATED MILK SLOWLY ON IT AND STIR UNTIL MIXTURE IS SMOOTH. IF NO ROE, MELT 1/4 C BUTTER AND STIR IN 1/4 C FLOUR AND GRADUALLY ADD 3 C MILK. HEAT UNTIL THICKENED. ADD 1/4 TSP. NUTMEG. ADD LOBSTER MEAT AND STOCK AND SIMMER FIVE MINUTES. REMOVE FROM HEAT AND STIR IN 1 C HOT (NOT BOILING) CREAM. SEASON WITH THYME, A TOUCH OF CAYENNE AND SHERRY (OPTIONAL). GARNISH WITH PARSLEY AND PAPRIKA.

CORN CHOWDER (2 QT)

- 1/2 LB. SALT PORK, DICED
- 2 MEDIUM ONIONS, CHOPPED
- 1/2 C CHOPPED CELERY AND TOPS
- 1/2 BAY LEAF
- 2 TBLSP. FLOUR
- 1 QT. WATER
- 1/4 C BUTTER
- 3 C DICED RAW POTATOES
- 1 CAN CREAM CORN
- 2 C EVAPORATED MILK
- SALT AND PEPPER
- 1 TBLSP. WORCESTERSHIRE
- 3 CHICKEN BOUILLON CUBES
- PARSLEY
- PAPRIKA

FRY UP PORK WITH ONION, CELERY AND BAY. REMOVE PORK. BLEND IN FLOUR - ADD 1 QT. WATER, BOUILLON AND POTATOES. SIMMER 15 MINUTES. ADD CORN AND MILK. HEAT AND ADD SALT, PEPPER, BUTTER AND WORCESTERSHIRE. GARNISH WITH PARSLEY AND PAPRIKA.

HADDOCK

Tomato Bisque (2 qt.)

Make 1 qt. medium white sauce, with ½ tsp. of dry mustard added. In a separate pan, heat 1 can (#303) peeled tomatoes and 1 can (#303) stewed tomatoes. When tomatoes and white sauce are both hot, add ½ tsp. baking soda to tomatoes and stir until froth subsides. Quickly blend white sauce and tomatoes. Season with 2 tblsp. parmesan cheese, ½ tsp. sweet basil and 2 tblsp. butter. Garnish with parsley.

Hearty Split Pea Soup (Serves 10)

- 1 ham bone and any ham scraps
- 1 pkg. (1 lb.) dried split peas
- 2 carrots, sliced
- 2 onions, chopped
- 7 c water
- ¼ tsp. allspice
- Salt and pepper to taste
- 2 tsp. Worcestershire
- ½ bay leaf
- ¼ tsp. celery salt
- ¼ tsp. onion salt
- ¼ tsp. garlic pwd.
- ½ c chopped celery leaves
- ¼ tsp. season-all
- Dash A-1 sauce

In a kettle, heat bone, peas, carrots, onions and celery leaves with water. Bring to a boil and add seasonings. Reduce heat, cover and simmer 45 minutes, or until peas are tender. Remove any meat from bone and return to soup. Discard bone. Add more water if needed. Adjust seasoning.

Lentil Soup

- 1 - 1 lb. pkg. lentils
- ¼ lb. bacon, diced
- 2 sliced onions
- 2 diced carrots
- 1½ qt. water
- 1 c sliced celery
- 8 oz. stewed tomatoes
- Salt, pepper to taste
- ½ tsp. thyme
- 2 bay leaves
- 1 lg. pared potato
- 1 ham bone - or Polish sausage
- 1 tblsp. lemon jce.
- Parsley

Saute bacon, onions and carrots. Add lentils, water, celery, tomatoes, salt, pepper, thyme, and bay. With medium grater,

GRATE IN POTATO. ADD HAM BONE. SIMMER, COVERED, 1 1/2 HR. REMOVE BAY LEAVES AND BONE, LEAVING IN ANY HAM SCRAPS. IF USING POLISH SAUSAGE, ADD IT NOW. HEAT AND ADJUST SEASONING. ADD LEMON JUICE JUST BEFORE SERVING. GARNISH WITH PARSLEY.

Pumpkin Soup (SERVES 8-10)

YOU MAY USE PUMPKIN, BUTTERNUT OR HUBBARD SQUASH. PEEL 2 1/2 LB. PUMPKIN OR SQUASH. SCRAPE OUT THE SEEDS, CUT IN CHUNKS AND BOIL IN SALTED WATER UNTIL TENDER. DRAIN, RESERVING WATER AND MASH THE PUMPKIN FINELY. ADD PUMPKIN WATER (OR CHICKEN BROTH) UNTIL IT'S A THICK PURÉE. ADD 2 CHOPPED CARROTS, 1 DICED STALK CELERY, 3 SLICES CHOPPED BACON, 1 LARGE CHOPPED ONION, AND 1 CHOPPED GREEN PEPPER. SIMMER UNTIL VEGETABLES ARE TENDER. ADD 1 TBLSP. FLOUR (MIXED TO A PASTE WITH WATER), 1/2 TSP. THYME, 1 C CANNED TOMATOES (OR CHOPPED FRESH), SALT AND PEPPER TO TASTE AND 2 TBLSP. BUTTER. HEAT 1/2 CAN EVAPORATED MILK AND ADD JUST BEFORE SERVING. GARNISH WITH FRESH CHOPPED PARSLEY.

Minestrone — A GREAT SOUP FOR LUNCH ON A COOL DAY. INGREDIENT AMOUNTS ARE FLEXIBLE, UTILIZING LEFT-OVERS.

FRY UP 3 CHOPPED SLICES BACON WITH 2 CHOPPED ONIONS, 1 CLOVE MINCED GARLIC, 2 CHOPPED POTATOES, 2 CHOPPED CARROTS AND 1/2 C DICED CELERY (FEW LEAVES TOO). ADD 1/4 C OLIVE OIL, 2 TSP. BASIL, 2 TBLSP. PARSLEY, 1/2 TSP. OREGANO, 1 C CHOPPED CABBAGE AND 1 C TOMATOES. ZUCCHINI MAY BE ADDED — EVEN EGGPLANT. ADD CONSOMME OR BEEF STOCK, AND BEANS. (USE DRIED WHITE BEANS THAT HAVE BEEN SOAKED AND COOKED, OR CANNED — WE'VE EVEN USED LEFT-OVERS FROM THE BEAN POTS). TOSS IN A HANDFUL OF MACARONI. SIMMER 10 MINUTES. TOP WITH PARMESAN AND PARSLEY.

HOT LUNCHEON DISHES

CHILI (FOR 10)

SOAK ½ PKG. RED KIDNEY BEANS OVERNIGHT. CHANGE THE WATER AND CHOP IN AN ONION AND ADD 1 MASHED CLOVE GARLIC. BRING TO A BOIL AND SIMMER UNTIL TENDER. DO NOT ADD SALT AT THIS TIME AS IT TOUGHENS THE BEANS. — OR YOU MAY USE A 20-OZ. CAN OF KIDNEY BEANS.   SAUTÉ 3 CHOPPED SLICES BACON WITH 1 CHOPPED ONION, 1 CRUSHED CLOVE GARLIC AND 1 LB. GROUND BEEF UNTIL BEEF IS BROWN. ADD 1 TBLSP. CHILI PWD., ½ TSP. CELERY SEED, ½ TSP. SEASON-ALL, AND SALT AND BLACK PEPPER TO TASTE. ADD 1 CAN (#2½) TOMATOES, 1 TBLSP. WORCESTERSHIRE AND 1 TBLSP. BUTTER. SIMMER 30 MINUTES AND ADD THE BEANS. SERVE WITH STEAMED RICE.

BEEF - NOODLE FOG CHASER

- 1 LB. NOODLES
- 5 SLICES BACON
- 2 LB. HAMBURGER
- 2 CHOPPED ONIONS
- 2 CLOVES GARLIC, MINCED
- 1 CHOPPED GREEN PEPPER
- 1 TBLSP. OREGANO
- 1 LARGE CAN TOMATOES
- 1-8 OZ CAN TOMATO SAUCE
- 1 CAN NIBLET CORN
- 1 TBLSP. CHILI PWD.
- SALT AND PEPPER
- 1 TBLSP. WORCESTERSHIRE
- 1 TBLSP. PARSLEY
- ½ LB. GRATED AMERICAN CHEESE

BROWN BACON (CHOPPED) AND ADD MEAT, ONIONS, GARLIC, GREEN PEPPER AND OREGANO. SIMMER UNTIL MEAT IS BROWN. ADD TOMATOES, TOMATO SAUCE AND CORN. ADD SALT AND PEPPER TO TASTE, CHILI PWD., WORCESTERSHIRE AND PARSLEY. SIMMER ONE HOUR. CHECK SEASONING. ADD COOKED NOODLES AND SPRINKLE CHEESE ON TOP. SERVE WITH HOT FRENCH BREAD.   SERVES 10

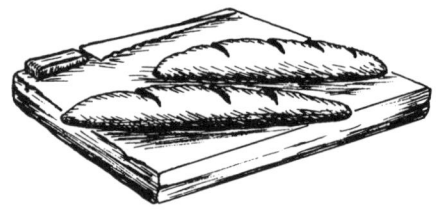

Spaghetti Sauce

SAUTÉ IN 3 TBLSP. OLIVE OIL – 1 C MINCED ONIONS, 1 MINCED CLOVE GARLIC, 1 TSP. OREGANO AND 1 LB. HAMBURGER. WHEN HAMBURGER IS BROWN, ADD 1 CAN (1 LB. 13 OZ.) ITALIAN PEELED TOMATOES, 2 8 OZ. CANS TOMATO SAUCE, 1 TSP. SALT, 1/4 TSP. PEPPER, 1 TSP. ONION SALT, 1 TSP. BASIL, 1 TBLSP. WORCESTERSHIRE AND 1 TSP. SUGAR. SIMMER ABOUT 1 HOUR. I LIKE TO STIR IN 1/4 C RED WINE.

IF TIME IS SHORT AND THE STOVE TOP IS IN DEMAND, A PKG. SPAGHETTI SAUCE IS USED, ADDING ONION, GARLIC AND THE GROUND BEEF.

Stir Fried Rice (for 6)

- 3 C COLD COOKED RICE
- 2 C SLIVERED MEAT (MAY BE STEAK, CHICKEN, VEAL OR A COMBINATION)
- 3 SLICES BACON, CHOPPED
- 3 EGGS
- 2 ONIONS, COARSELY CHOPPED
- 1 GREEN PEPPER, COARSELY CHOPPED
- 1 MINCED CLOVE GARLIC
- 2 CELERY STALKS, SLICED
- 1 CAN WATER CHESTNUTS, CHOP
- 1 C BEAN SPROUTS
- SOY SAUCE
- CHINESE NOODLES
- SWEET AND SOUR SAUCE

MARINATE MEAT IN TERIYAKI OR SOY SAUCE 1/2 HR. SAUTÉ ONIONS, PEPPERS, CELERY AND GARLIC IN 2 TBLSP. OIL 5 MINUTES. SET ASIDE. SAUTÉ MEAT WITH BACON A FEW MINUTES. ADD TO VEGETABLES. SCRAMBLE EGGS IN OIL UNTIL FIRM. SLIVER AND ADD TO MEAT. STIR-FRY RICE IN HOT OIL, ADDING SOY SAUCE AS YOU DO (ABOUT 1/4 C). MIX ALL BUT CHINESE NOODLES AND SWEET AND SOUR, WHICH ARE SERVED AT TABLE AS TOPPINGS.

拓 本

Red Flannel Hash   (Serves 6)

- 1½ c chopped corned beef
- 1½ c chopped boiled potatoes
- 1½ c chopped boiled beets
- 1 medium onion, minced
- ¼ c milk
- Salt and pepper to taste
- 1 tsp. Worcestershire
- 2 tblsp. butter

Add all ingredients to the butter in a hot frying pan. Stir until heated. Cook until the mixture is brown and crusty underneath. Fold as an omelet. Garnish with parsley.

Pizza   (2 – 12" pizzas)

Dough:
- 1 c warm water
- 1 pkg. dry yeast
- 2 tblsp. shortening
- ½ tsp. salt
- 4 c flour
- 2 tsp. oil

Dissolve yeast in warm water. Add shortening, salt and half of flour. Gradually add the rest of the flour and turn out on a floured board to knead until smooth. Place in an oiled bowl, turn dough to coat, cover and let rise until double. Punch down and knead a few minutes. Roll into 2 circles (or to fit your pans). Fit into pans leaving an edge up the sides. Fill as desired.

Pizza Sauce

In 1 tblsp. oil, saute ¼ c chopped onion and 1 minced clove garlic until soft. Add 1 can (1 lb. 3 oz) whole tomatoes (mash tomatoes with a fork), 1-8 oz. can tomato sauce, 1 bay leaf, 1 tsp. salt, 1 tsp. sugar, 1 tsp. oregano and ¼ tsp. pepper. Simmer 30 minutes.   Spread on pizza dough.

Filling Variations: **Anchovy** – Arrange anchovies (2 oz. can) on sauce. Cover with 1 lb. sliced mozzarella cheese.

Sausage: Place browned, drained sausage on sauce and cover with 1 lb. sliced mozzarella cheese.

Onion – Green Pepper: Slice 2 onions and 1 green pepper thinly – spread on sauce and cover with 1 c parmesan cheese – or mozzarella. Sliced <u>salami</u> is good and <u>mushrooms</u> are too!

Oven 450°. Bake 25 minutes.

Turkey or Chicken Loaf   (Makes 1 Loaf)

2 c diced or ground cooked chicken or turkey
2 c soft bread crumbs   1 tblsp. minced parsley
1/4 c chopped onion   1/2 tsp. salt   1/4 tsp. paprika
2 tblsp. chopped pimiento   3 eggs, beaten   2 c milk
1/2 c chopped celery   2 tblsp. butter

Combine all the ingredients and mix well. You may add 1/2 c mushrooms or serve with mushroom soup as a sauce. Pour into a greased 9 x 5" loaf pan. Bake at 350° about 40 minutes. Serve with mushroom, cheese or egg sauce.

Pineapple-Glazed Ham Loaf

1 tblsp. butter   milk   1 tblsp. chopped parsley
1/3 c brown sugar   1 egg, beat   1 tblsp. grated onion
1/2 tsp. ground cloves   1 c Pepperidge Farm stuffing mix
1 can (13 1/2 oz.) crushed pineapple   1/4 c chopped green pepper
1 lb. cooked, ground ham   1 lb. hamburger   1 tblsp. mustard

Melt butter in a 9 x 5" loaf pan. Mix brown sugar and cloves and sprinkle into pan. Drain pineapple (save juice) and spread on sugar. In bowl, combine remaining ingredients, using pineapple juice and enough milk to make 1 c. Turn meat mix into pan, pressing firmly. Bake at 350° 1 1/4 hours. Drain any liquid and invert on a platter to serve.

Meat Loaf

2 lb. hamburger   1 c tomato juice   salt and pepper
3 slices bread, crumbed   1/4 c catsup   to taste
1/2 c milk   1 tblsp. Worcestershire   1/2 c chopped
1 tblsp. parsley   1 chopped onion   green pepper
1 pkg. Liptons dry onion soup   1 egg   1/2 tsp. Season-All

Mix all together and pack in a 9 x 5" loaf pan. Bake at 350° 1 hour covered with foil and 1/2 hour uncovered. Top with cheese, tomatoes, sweet and sour — whatever you wish!

SALADS

TANGY SLAW (SERVES 4)

3 C SHREDDED CABBAGE ½ C SOUR CREAM 1 ½ TBLSP. SUGAR
2 TBLSP. GRATED ONION 1 ½ TSP. SALT ¼ TSP. PAPRIKA
1 TSP. CELERY SEED DASH CAYENNE 4 TBLSP. VINEGAR
½ C MAYONNAISE 1 TSP. DRY MUSTARD 1 TSP. CARAWAY SEED

MIX ALL TOGETHER AND LET SIT AN HOUR OR SO BEFORE SERVING. DILL SEED MAY BE USED IN PLACE OF CARAWAY IF YOU WISH. GRATED CARROTS MAY BE ADDED FOR COLOR.

PINEAPPLE SLAW (SERVES 4)

3 C SHREDDED CABBAGE ¼ C CHOPPED MARASCHINO CHERRIES
1 C MINIATURE MARSHMALLOWS ½ C MAYONNAISE
1 - 17 OZ. CAN DRAINED CRUSHED PINEAPPLE ½ C WHIPPED CREAM

MIX ALL TOGETHER AND SERVE.

ANDREA'S WILTED SPINACH (SERVES 4)

1 LB. SPINACH 2 TBLSP. SUGAR
4 SLICES BACON, DICED ½ TSP. SALT
⅓ C VINEGAR DASH PEPPER
1 HARD BOILED EGG, CHOPPED ⅓ C WATER
¾ TSP. DRY MUSTARD

CLEAN SPINACH AND BREAK INTO LARGE PIECES IN A BOWL. FRY BACON, DRAIN AND RESERVE. MIX AND HEAT VINEGAR, WATER, SUGAR, MUSTARD, SALT AND PEPPER. STIR EGG AND BACON INTO SPINACH. POUR HOT VINEGAR MIXTURE OVER SPINACH JUST BEFORE SERVING.

RICE SALAD   (SERVES 4)

- 2 c COOKED RICE
- 1/4 c SALAD OIL
- 1/4 c WINE VINEGAR
- 6 WATER CHESTNUTS, CHOPPED
- 1/2 c MINCED PARSLEY
- 1/4 c MINCED GREEN ONION
- 1/2 GREEN PEPPER, CHOPPED
- 1/2 c CHOPPED CELERY
- 1 TSP. MIXED HERBS
- SALT AND PEPPER

STIR OIL AND VINEGAR INTO RICE WHILE HOT. COOL AND ADD THE REST OF THE INGREDIENTS. SEASON TO TASTE AND DRESS WITH 1/2 c GREEN GODDESS DRESSING.

RICE AND BEAN SALAD   (SERVES 6)

- 1/2 c SALAD OIL
- 1/2 c WINE VINEGAR
- 2 TBLSP. SUGAR
- 1 TSP. SALT
- 1 c DICED CELERY
- 1/2 GREEN PEPPER, CHOPPED
- 1/2 TSP. PEPPER
- 1 CAN RED KIDNEY BEANS, DRAINED
- 1 CAN CUT GREEN BEANS, DRAINED
- 1 MEDIUM RED ONION, THINLY SLICED
- 3 PIMIENTOS, DICED
- 2 c COOKED COLD RICE

BLEND OIL, VINEGAR, SUGAR, SALT AND PEPPER. IN A BOWL, MIX CELERY, GREEN PEPPER, KIDNEY BEANS, GREEN BEANS, ONION, PIMIENTO AND RICE. POUR OIL-VINEGAR MIXTURE OVER VEGETABLES AND REFRIGERATE A COUPLE OF HOURS BEFORE SERVING.

POTATO SALAD IDEAS

BOIL UP POTATOES ENOUGH FOR YOUR GROUP. DRAIN, AND WHILE POTATOES ARE HOT, POUR OVER FRENCH OR ITALIAN DRESSING AND MIX GENTLY. COOL. THEN ADD MINCED ONION, CHOPPED CELERY AND GREEN PEPPER. SEASON WITH SALT, PEPPER, SEASON ALL, FINES HERBS, PARSLEY, MUSTARD AND MAYONNAISE. DILL SEED IS AN INTERESTING ADDITION. GARNISH WITH CHOPPED HARD BOILED EGGS AND CRUMBLED BACON.

ROAST BEEF SALAD

(COURTESY OF THE "HARVEY GAMAGE") — A GREAT USE FOR LEFT-OVER ROAST BEEF. PROPORTIONS ARE A LITTLE LOOSE, DEPENDING ON THE AMOUNT OF BEEF YOU HAVE. MIX CHUNKS OF COOKED ROAST BEEF WITH CHOPPED TOMATOES, CHOPPED ONION AND PARSLEY. MAKE A DRESSING OF 2/3 C SALAD OIL, 3 TBLSP. RED WINE VINEGAR AND 1½ TBLSP. DIJON MUSTARD. SHAKE UP AND TOSS WITH SALAD. SALT AND PEPPER TO TASTE. DEPENDING ON QUANTITIES INVOLVED, YOU MIGHT NEED MORE (OR LESS) DRESSING.

GREEN SALADS

THE USUAL ASSORTMENT OF GREENS ARE BROKEN UP AND ADDITIONS DEPEND ON WHAT IS ON HAND AND MOOD — CUCUMBERS, TOMATO WEDGES, RADISHES, GREEN PEPPER, CARROTS. IF WE'VE SPROUTED MUNG BEANS OR ALFALFA SEEDS, THEY'RE ADDED. TRY ADDING A HANDFUL OF SUNFLOWER SEEDS. RAW SLICED MUSHROOMS ARE SUPER. SEASONED CROUTONS ARE KEPT ON THE SHELF AND TOSSED ON AT THE LAST MINUTE. WE SOMETIMES USE GOOD SEASONS DRESSING MIXES, OR MAKE OUR OWN. HERE ARE TWO TO TRY:

TOMATO FRENCH DRESSING

1 CAN TOMATO SOUP	½ C VINEGAR	1 TBLSP. DRY MUSTARD
1 CAN SALAD OIL	1/8 TSP. GARLIC PWD.	SALT AND PEPPER
1 C SUGAR	2 TBLSP. CELERY SEED	

BEAT ALL TOGETHER WELL WITH A WHISK OR SHAKE IN A JAR.

GARLIC DRESSING

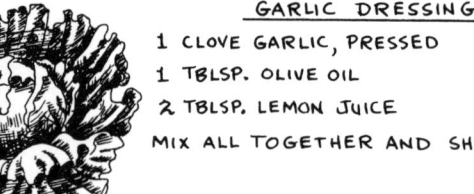

1 CLOVE GARLIC, PRESSED	1 TSP. SALT
1 TBLSP. OLIVE OIL	1 TSP. ACCENT
2 TBLSP. LEMON JUICE	6 SHAKES TABASCO

MIX ALL TOGETHER AND SHAKE WELL.

Fruit Salads

Summertime in New England gives an abundance of fresh fruits. Combinations depend on what's "in", but there are melons, plums, pears, grapes, citrus, cherries, apples and berries. Most weeks fruit is heaped in a scalloped watermelon rind to serve with a <u>DRESSING</u> of:

1 c sour cream	1 tblsp. lemon juice
1 c whipped cream	1 tblsp. pwd. sugar
½ tsp. cinnamon	

Orange-Onion Salad

Don't knock it until you try it! - Orange sections on a bed of lettuce with red onion rings. Serve with French dressing.

Lime-Cheese Mold

1 pkg. lime jello	2 c crushed pineapple	2 tsp. horseradish
1 pkg. lemon jello	1 c milk	1 c cottage cheese
2 c hot water	1 c chopped nuts	1 c mayonnaise

Dissolve jello in hot water and let cool. Add drained pineapple. Combine milk, nuts, cheese and mayonnaise. When jello is partially set, mix the two together. Add horseradish. Place in a mold and chill until firm.

Notes

MEATS FOWL FISH

There are wonderful meats to work with on "Adventure". Purchased from a hotel supply chain, the turkey, lamb, pork and beef are boned, netted, and even have self-timers built in. It's hard to go wrong!

TURKEY – is pre-cooked turkey breast which needs only to be brushed with butter and baked until good and hot.

LAMB is best with slivers of garlic buried inside, brushed with a mixture of Worcestershire and lemon juice. Season with salt, pepper, basil, marjoram, thyme and onion.

PORK is nice with the following sauce to baste with as it roasts: 1/2 c Madeira wine, 1 tsp. salt, dash pepper, and 1/8 tsp. ground nutmeg. Brush meat often. The gravy made from these pan drippings is something special.

BEEF: Brush with Worcestershire and season with salt, pepper, celery seed, season-all and rosemary. I like to chop an onion into the pan towards the end of the roasting.

YORKSHIRE PUDDING (serve with roast beef)

Have all ingredients at room temperature. Sift 1 c flour with 1/2 tsp. salt. Make a well and pour in 1/2 c milk. Stir in. Beat 2 eggs until fluffy and mix in. Add 1/2 c milk. Beat well until large bubbles rise. This may now stand in the refrigerator for an hour, covered. Beat again. In a 9 x 12" ovenproof dish, melt beef drippings (1/4"). Pan should be smoking hot (muffin tins can be used). Pour in batter. Bake at 400° 20 minutes, and at 350° for 10-15 minutes longer. Serve immediately.

FISH: Fresh haddock is so good! Brushed with lemon butter, sprinkled with paprika and baked at 350° about 20 minutes until it flakes easily with a fork. Food fit for the gods!

Here are a few ways with fish that we're fond of:

FISH FLORENTINE (SERVES 6)

3 C COOKED FISH   1/3 C BUTTER   3 SHAKES TABASCO
3 C MILK   DASH OF WINE   1 TSP. SALT   1 C GRATED CHEDDAR CHEESE
1/3 C FLOUR   1 TSP. MUSTARD   2 PKG. DRAINED SPINACH

MAKE A SAUCE WITH BUTTER, FLOUR, MILK, MUSTARD, SALT, TABASCO AND WINE. PLACE SPINACH IN A CASSEROLE, THEN FISH. POUR SAUCE OVER, SPRINKLE WITH SLIVERED ALMONDS, TOP WITH CHEESE AND BAKE 30 MINUTES AT 350°.

MACADAMIA NUT FISH (SERVES 6)

BAKE OR SAUTÉ 2 LB. FISH FILLETS. POUR THE FOLLOWING SAUCE OVER FISH AND SERVE SPRINKLED WITH PARSLEY.

SAUCE: MIX 2 TSP. CORNSTARCH IN 2 TBLSP. WATER. ADD TO 1 C RICH CHICKEN BROTH, ADD THE JUICE FROM 1/2 LEMON, 1/4 C HOLLANDAISE AND 1/2 C CRUSHED MACADAMIA NUTS.

BETH'S "AH SO" FISH (FOR 6)

BAKE 2 LB. FISH FILLETS (SEE PAGE 84) AND SERVE WITH THE FOLLOWING SAUCE POURED OVER THE FISH. HEAP CHINESE NOODLES AROUND THE EDGES.

SAUCE: SAUTÉ 1/2 C MUSHROOM PIECES, 1/3 C CHOPPED ONIONS, 1/4 C EACH CHOPPED GREEN AND RED PEPPERS (IF RED PEPPERS ARE NOT AVAILABLE, CHOPPED RED PIMIENTOS MAY BE ADDED TO SAUCE LATER.) ADD 1 CAN CREAM OF MUSHROOM SOUP, 1/2 CAN MILK, 1/4 C SHERRY. SEASON TO TASTE WITH SALT, PEPPER AND GARLIC.

OVEN FRIED FISH (SERVES 6)

2 LB. FISH FILLETS	1/4 TSP. TARRAGON	1 TSP. WORCESTERSHIRE
1/4 C EVAPORATED MILK	1/4 TSP. DILL WEED	1/4 C BUTTER
1 TSP. SALT	1/2 C PROGRESSO SEASONED BREAD CRUMBS	

MIX MILK, SALT, TARRAGON, DILL AND WORCESTERSHIRE IN A FLAT DISH. PLACE CRUMBS IN ANOTHER. DIP FISH IN MILK, THEN ROLL IN CRUMBS. PLACE FILLETS IN AN OILED SHALLOW PAN IN A SINGLE LAYER. DRIZZLE MELTED BUTTER OVER FISH. BAKE AT 500° 20 MINUTES UNTIL GOLDEN AND EASILY FLAKED. SERVE WITH <u>MUSTARD SAUCE</u>: SAUTÉ IN 1/3 C BUTTER, 1/3 C MINCED ONION AND 1 MINCED CLOVE GARLIC. WHEN ONION IS TENDER, ADD 1/2 TSP. SALT, DASH PEPPER, 2 TSP. WORCESTERSHIRE, 1 1/2 TSP. PREPARED MUSTARD AND 3 TBLSP. CHILI SAUCE. HEAT.

BAKED STUFFED HADDOCK (SERVES 6)

MAKE UP A VEGETABLE STUFFING.* SAUTÉ IN 3 TBLSP. BUTTER — 1/2 C ONION (CHOPPED), 1/4 C CHOPPED CELERY, 1/4 C CHOPPED GREEN PEPPER, AND 1/2 C CHOPPED MUSHROOMS. STIR IN 2 C SOFT BREAD CRUMBS, 1 TSP. SALT, DASH OF PEPPER, 1/4 TSP. TARRAGON AND 1/4 TSP. DILL WEED. PLACE 2 LBS. OF HADDOCK FILLETS IN A LAYER IN A BUTTERED SHALLOW PAN. SPRINKLE WITH LEMON JUICE. SPREAD STUFFING OVER FISH AND COVER WITH PEELED, SLICED TOMATOES. BAKE AT 375° ABOUT 40 MINUTES.

* SEE P. 71

CHICKEN WAYS:

<u>OVEN FRIED</u>: COAT CHICKEN BREASTS AND THIGHS WITH EVAPORATED MILK, FRENCH DRESSING OR MAYONNAISE. ROLL IN SEASONED CRUMBS AND BAKE AT 350° FOR 1-1 1/2 HOURS.

<u>SHERRIED CHICKEN</u>: BAKE CHICKEN PARTS IN A 350° OVEN ONE HOUR AND THEN POUR OVER A MIXTURE OF 1 CAN CREAM OF MUSHROOM SOUP AND 1/2 C SHERRY. BAKE 1/2 HOUR MORE.

COUNTRY CHICKEN

COAT CHICKEN PARTS IN SEASONED FLOUR AND SAUTÉ IN BACON GREASE UNTIL BROWN. PLACE IN A CASSEROLE. IN 3 TBLSP. BUTTER, SAUTÉ 1 ONION, COARSELY CUT, AND 1 GREEN PEPPER, COARSELY CUT. ADD 3 TBLSP. CURRY PWD. AND LET COOK UP A MINUTE. ADD 1 LARGE CAN (#2½) TOMATOES. POUR OVER CHICKEN. ADD ½ C RAISINS AND BAKE AT 350° ONE HOUR.

MANDARIN CHICKEN

1 TO 3 CHICKENS, QUARTERED	2 TBLSP. SOY	2 TBLSP. SUGAR
1 CAN MANDARIN ORANGES	1 C TOMATO SAUCE	PINEAPPLE CHUNKS
⅓ C VINEGAR	1 CLOVE GARLIC, MASHED	GREEN PEPPER
2 TBLSP. BUTTER	½ TSP. GINGER	SQUARES

BAKE CHICKEN AT 350°. BRUSH WITH BUTTER AND BASTE WITH THE FOLLOWING SAUCE: MIX MANDARIN JUICE, TOMATO SAUCE, VINEGAR, BUTTER, SOY, GARLIC, AND GINGER. BRING TO A BOIL. BEFORE SERVING, ADD SUGAR, ORANGES, PINEAPPLE AND PEPPERS. ADD DRIPPINGS FROM CHICKEN. STIR AND POUR OVER CHICKEN PARTS.

Ham

THE HAMS WORKED WITH ARE BONELESS AND PRE-COOKED — ALL READY FOR GLAZING. SCORE HAM ⅛" DEEP IN DIAGONAL CUTS, STUD WITH CLOVES AND BRUSH WITH A GLAZE.

ORANGE GLAZE: MIX ½ C STRAINED ORANGE MARMALADE WITH 1 C DARK CORN SYRUP AND 2 TSP. DRY MUSTARD.

MAPLE: MIX ¾ C MAPLE SYRUP WITH ¾ C DARK CORN SYRUP AND 2 TBLSP. PREPARED MUSTARD.

CRUST: MIX 1⅓ C BROWN SUGAR, 2 TSP. DRY MUSTARD, ⅓ C FINE DRY BREAD CRUMBS AND 3 TBLSP. RED WINE OR CIDAR VINEGAR. PAT THIS MIXTURE ON HAM AND THEN STUD WITH CLOVES.

BAKE HAM AT 375° UNTIL BROWNED AND HOT THROUGH. SLICE AND SERVE WITH RAISIN SAUCE OR FRUIT COMPOTE.

Raisin Sauce

In a saucepan, mix 1/4 c brown sugar, 1 1/2 tblsp. cornstarch, 1/8 tsp. salt and 1 c cider or beer. Stir in 1/4 c raisins, 1/4 tsp. cloves and 1/2 tsp. cinnamon. Cook and stir until thick and clear. Add 1 tblsp. butter.

Fruit Compote

Slice up in a pan: 8 small peaches, apples or pears (or a combination)
Add:
- 2/3 c red wine
- 2/3 c sugar
- 1/2 stick cinnamon
- 1/8 tsp. salt
- 4 whole cloves
- 1/2 thin sliced lemon

Bring to a boil, lower the heat and simmer 15 minutes. You may vary the fruit — using dried, fresh or canned.

Corned Beef

Cover a 5 lb. piece of corned beef with boiling water. Add 1 mashed clove garlic, 1 quartered onion, 2 bay leaves, 2 whole cloves, 10 black peppercorns and 1/4 tsp. mustard seed. Simmer 4 hours. Serve with:

Horseradish Sauce

1 c cream sauce   2 tblsp. whipping cream   1 tblsp. vinegar
3 tblsp. horseradish   1 tsp. sugar   1 tsp. dry mustard
Mix all together and bring to a boil.

New England Boiled Dinner

After corned beef has simmered in the stock 4 hours, remove meat and add the following to the broth:

   3 small parsnips   3 large yellow turnips
   6 large carrots   8 small onions

Simmer 15 minutes and add 6 medium potatoes, quartered. Simmer 15 minutes more and add a head of cabbage, cut into wedges. Ten minutes for the cabbage. Reheat the meat in the stock and serve with the vegetables heaped around the corned beef.

Meat Notes

VEGETABLES

ARTICHOKES

Canned artichoke hearts give an elegant touch to salads, but they are also a fine accompaniment to a meat course when served as follows:

Artichoke Parmesan Casserole (serves 6)

2 cans artichoke hearts, drained   Parmesan cheese
½ cup seasoned bread crumbs   Salad oil

Rinse artichoke hearts, drain and cut in quarters. Sprinkle with olive oil and parmesan cheese. Cover with bread crumbs stirred in melted butter. Bake 30 minutes at 350°.

GREEN BEANS

We prefer undercooked fresh vegetables, as the flavor and color are so much nicer. Green beans lend themselves to endless variations. ① Cook with onion and bacon pieces or ham bits.

② Top cooked beans with cream of mushroom soup and cover with canned french fried onion rings.

③ Sauté ¼ c slivered almonds in ¼ c butter until brown and stir into cooked beans. Salt and pepper to taste.

④ Add chopped mushrooms and/or water chestnuts. Season to taste.

SWEET SOUR BEANS

Cook 1 lb. green beans until barely tender. Fry up 3 chopped slices bacon and 2 tblsp. chopped onion. Remove bacon when crisp and add to pan 1 tblsp. wine vinegar, 1 tblsp. sugar and ½ tsp. salt. Pour over beans and add bacon.

Maine Baked Beans

1 LB. JACOB CATTLE BEANS (OR YELLOW, PEA OR KIDNEY)
1/4 LB. SALT PORK   1/3 C MOLASSES   1/3 C CATSUP
    1 MEDIUM ONION   2 TSP. SALT   1/4 TSP. PEPPER
2 TBLSP. BROWN SUGAR   1 TSP. DRY MUSTARD   1 C HOT WATER
1 TBLSP. WORCESTERSHIRE   1/2 TSP. GARLIC PWD.

YOU MAY USE PART MAPLE SYRUP FOR THE MOLASSES. SOAK THE BEANS OVERNIGHT IN WATER TO COVER. THEN PARBOIL UNTIL THE SKINS CRACK WHEN BLOWN UPON. (1/2 - 1 HOUR) QUARTER THE ONION AND PUT IN THE BOTTOM OF THE BEAN POT. ADD THE BEANS. CUT THROUGH RIND OF THE SALT PORK AND PLACE ON TOP OF BEANS. MIX REMAINING INGREDIENTS AND POUR OVER BEANS. BAKE AT 300° - 4 TO 6 HOURS. ADD WATER IF NECESSARY. —THE WOOD STOVE IS PERFECT FOR THIS DISH... EITHER IN THE BOTTOM OF THE OVEN OR ON THE BACK OF THE STOVE.

Beets

① SEASON BEETS WITH SALT, PEPPER, PARSLEY AND BUTTER.
② SEASON WITH BUTTER, BROWN SUGAR AND GRATED ORANGE RIND.

Beets and Sour Cream

COMBINE AND HEAT TOGETHER:
- 3 C COOKED SLICED BEETS
- 1/2 C SOUR CREAM
- 1 TBLSP. CHOPPED CHIVES
- SALT AND PEPPER
- 1 TBLSP. HORSERADISH
- 1 TBLSP. PARSLEY

Harvard Beets

3 C COOKED, SLICED BEETS   1/4 TSP. PEPPER
1/2 C SUGAR   1/4 TSP. CLOVES   1/2 C CIDAR VINEGAR
1/2 TSP. SALT   1 TBLSP. CORNSTARCH   2 TBLSP. BUTTER

STIR TOGETHER IN A SAUCEPAN — SUGAR, CORNSTARCH, SALT, CLOVES AND VINEGAR. COOK AND STIR UNTIL MIXTURE IS THICK AND CLEAR. ADD BEETS AND BUTTER. THE ADDITION OF A COUPLE OF TBLSP. OF ORANGE MARMALADE IS INTERESTING.

Broccoli and Brussels Sprouts

We treat both of these vegetables much the same. Cooked only until tender-crisp, simply add salt, pepper, butter and a squeeze of lemon juice. Sometimes they're served with a cheese or hollandaise sauce.

<u>Brussels Sprouts</u> may be varied by mixing in chestnuts or walnuts and topping with buttered bread crumbs.

Jiffy Hollandaise   (1½ c)

Heat 1 c mayonnaise or salad dressing in the top of a double boiler, stirring. Remove from heat and fold in ¼ c heavy cream, whipped and ½ tblsp. snipped chives. Stir until blended.

Hollandaise

Beat well 2 egg yolks (or 1 whole egg). Add salt, pepper, ¼ tsp. dry mustard, dash of cayenne (or tabasco) and a squirt of lemon juice. Melt up ½ lb. butter. Take from flame. Add a bit of butter to egg, beating with a whisk all the while. Beat-beat as you drip in butter. When it is all blended, you may need a little more lemon.

Cabbage

<u>Braised White</u> — Fry 3 bacon slices, drain and crumble. Toss 2 lb. fine shredded cabbage in bacon fat. Add 1½ tsp. salt, dash pepper and 3 tblsp. white wine vinegar. Cook 3 minutes.

<u>Cabbage in Mustard Sauce</u> — Shred a small head of cabbage. Sauté it lightly in butter or bacon drippings. Add ½ tsp. salt, ¼ tsp. paprika, ½ tsp. caraway seed, and 2 tblsp. minced onion. Place in a greased baking dish. Pour over 1½ c sour cream that has been mixed with 1 tblsp. mustard. Bake at 375° for 20 minutes. (Serves 4)

RED CABBAGE

2 LB. HEAD RED CABBAGE   1/4 TSP. SALT
4 CHOPPED SLICES BACON   1/2 C RED WINE
1/4 C CHOPPED ONION   1/4 TSP. CARAWAY SEED
2 APPLES   2 TBLSP. HONEY

SAUTÉ BACON AND ONION. ADD SHREDDED CABBAGE, COVER AND COOK TEN MINUTES. ADD APPLES (SLICED), CARAWAY, SALT, WINE AND HONEY. COVER AND SIMMER AN HOUR.

CARROTS

GRATE CARROTS (1 PER PERSON) AND A LITTLE ONION. STIR-FRY QUICKLY IN BUTTER IN A HOT SKILLET. ADD SALT AND PEPPER TO TASTE... NO MORE THAN 3 MINUTES COOKING!

CRAZY CARROTS

COOK 2 BUNCHES OF SMALL CARROTS IN ORANGE JUICE, 1/4 TSP. SALT AND 6 TBLSP. WATER UNTIL TENDER-CRISP. DRAIN. MELT 1/4 C BUTTER AND ADD 2 TBLSP. SUGAR AND 2 TBLSP. COINTREAU. ADD CARROTS AND COOK UNTIL GLAZED, TURNING. SERVE WITH COCONUT AS A GARNISH IF YOU WISH.

DILL WEED OR SEED IS LOVELY ADDED TO CARROTS WITH SALT, PEPPER AND BUTTER.

GOOD COMBO - CARROTS, MUSHROOMS, CHIVES AND ARTICHOKE HEARTS. SEASON WITH SALT AND PEPPER AND TOP WITH BUTTERED BREAD CRUMBS. BAKE AT 350° FOR 20 MINUTES.

GINGER CARROTS: SAUTÉ CHOPPED ONION IN BUTTER AND ADD TO COOKED, DRAINED CARROTS. ADD BROWN SUGAR, CHOPPED PRESERVED GINGER - HEAT AND STIR IN A COUPLE TBLSP. RUM. CHEERS!

CAULIFLOWER IS SO GOOD RAW, IT SEEMS A SHAME TO COOK IT. THE SECRET IS— NEVER OVER-COOK!

NOTE
STEAM FLOWERETS (OR WHOLE HEAD) WITH THE JUICE OF ½ LEMON. THIS WILL HELP KEEP IT WHITE.

CHINESE CAULIFLOWER

COARSELY GRATE A HEAD OF CAULIFLOWER. HEAT ¼ C BUTTER IN A LARGE SKILLET, AND QUICKLY SAUTÉ CAULIFLOWER (ABOUT 3 MINUTES). SEASON WITH SALT, PEPPER AND JUICE FROM ½ A LEMON. TO SERVE, SPRINKLE WITH PARMESAN CHEESE OR PAPRIKA.

SESAME CAULIFLOWER (SERVES 6)

COOK CAULIFLOWER (BROKEN UP) UNTIL TENDER-CRISP. (1 HEAD). DRAIN AND SET ASIDE. IN A SAUCEPAN, TOAST 2 TBLSP. SESAME SEED UNTIL BROWN, SHAKING PAN. PUT ON PAPER TOWEL. IN SAUCEPAN, MELT 2 TBLSP. BUTTER, STIR IN 2 TBLSP. FLOUR. GRADUALLY STIR IN 1 C CHICKEN BROTH AND COOK, STIRRING, UNTIL THICK. GENTLY STIR IN 2 TSP. LEMON JUICE, ½ TSP. SALT AND THE CAULIFLOWER. SPRINKLE WITH SESAME SEED.

<u>WITH ALMONDS</u>: BROWN CHOPPED BLANCHED ALMONDS IN HOT BUTTER. POUR OVER COOKED CAULIFLOWER HEAD AND SEASON WITH SALT AND PEPPER.
<u>WITH HOLLANDAISE</u>: SERVE HOT CAULIFLOWER WITH HOLLANDAISE.
<u>WITH CHEESE SAUCE</u>: SERVE HOT CAULIFLOWER WITH A CREAM SAUCE TO WHICH YOU HAVE ADDED EITHER GRATED SWISS OR AMERICAN CHEESE. GARNISH WITH PARSLEY OR CHIVES OR BUTTERED TOASTED BREAD CRUMBS.

(OVEN 350°) CAULIFLOWER PAPRIKA (SERVES 6)

PLACE COOKED FLOWERETS FROM 1 HEAD IN A BUTTERED CASSEROLE. SAUTÉ ¼ C CHOPPED GREEN PEPPER IN 2 TBLSP. BUTTER 3 MINUTES. ADD 2 TBLSP. FLOUR, ½ TSP. SALT AND ½ TSP. PAPRIKA. STIR IN 1 C MILK AND COOK UNTIL THICK. TAKE FROM FIRE AND ADD 1 C SOUR CREAM. POUR OVER CAULIFLOWER. CRUMBLE 1 - 3 OZ. PKG. CREAM CHEESE ON SAUCE. BAKE 20 MINUTES.

CORN

For fresh, sweet corn, we like to pour boiling water over the ears, add a tsp. of sugar (for 6 ears) and boil them four to ten minutes, depending on the age of the corn.

CREAMY FRESH CORN

- 7 or 8 ears corn
- 1/3 – 1/2 c butter
- 2 tblsp. flour
- 1 tblsp. sugar
- 1 tsp. season salt
- 1 tsp. grated onion
- 1/2 c milk
- 1/2 c light cream
- pepper or nutmeg

Slash through corn kernels with a small, sharp knife and scrape the kernels from the cob with the back of the knife. Melt butter in a skillet and stir in onion, corn and flour. Add sugar, salt and milk. Cover and cook slowly about ten minutes. Stir in cream just before serving. Sprinkle with pepper or nutmeg.

CASCO CORN PUDDING
(Serves 6-8)

- 2 c milk
- 1/4 c sugar
- 6 eggs, well beaten
- 1/4 c minced onion
- 1 c cracker crumbs
- 2 tblsp. flour
- 2 cans (16 oz.) creamed corn
- 1/2 c butter

Mix milk, sugar, eggs, onion, crumbs and flour. Beat well. Stir in corn. Melt 1/4 c butter and add. Pour into a buttered shallow baking dish. Dot with 1/4 c butter and bake at 350° 45 minutes. Allow to set a few minutes before serving. If you like, top with grated cheese and/or chopped parsley.

SPEEDY CORN RELISH (1 1/2 c)

- 2 c drained corn kernels
- 1/4 c chopped green pepper
- 1 small onion, chopped
- 1/3 c sweet pickle relish
- 1/4 tsp. celery seed
- 1/2 tsp. salt
- 1/2 tsp. dry mustard
- 2 tblsp. wine vinegar
- 2 tblsp. corn syrup
- 1 canned pimiento — chopped.
- dash pepper

Combine all in saucepan and simmer 5 minutes. Refrigerate.

CORN-TOMATO-PEPPER CASSEROLE (SERVES 8-10)

1 SMALL GREEN PEPPER	1/4 TSP. PEPPER	2 C CHOPPED TOMATOES
1/2 C CHOPPED ONION	1/2 TSP. DRY MUSTARD	2 TSP. SUGAR
1/4 C BUTTER	2 C MILK	1 C HERB STUFFING CROUTONS
1/4 C FLOUR	2 CANS (1 LB.) WHOLE KERNEL CORN, DRAINED	
2 TSP. SALT		2 EGGS, BEATEN

CHOP PEPPER AND SAUTÉ WITH ONION IN BUTTER UNTIL SOFT. ADD FLOUR, SALT, PEPPER AND MUSTARD. COOK AND STIR UNTIL BLENDED. GRADUALLY STIR IN MILK AND COOK UNTIL THICK AND SMOOTH. REMOVE FROM HEAT AND STIR IN CORN, TOMATOES, SUGAR AND CROUTONS. STIR IN EGGS. POUR INTO A GREASED 2 QT. CASSEROLE. BAKE AT 350° FOR 45-60 MINUTES. YOU MIGHT LIKE TO TOP THIS WITH BUTTERED CRUMBS OR GRATED CHEESE.

YELLOW VEGETABLE CASSEROLE (SERVES 6)

1 C CORN (CUT FROM 2 EARS)	1 C CHEESE, GRATED
1 SMALL HEAD CAULIFLOWER, CUT UP	BROWN RICE (FOR 6)
1/2 HEAD CABBAGE, CUT UP	2 CLOVES GARLIC, MINCED
2 LARGE CARROTS, CUT UP	1 TSP. SALT 1 C MILK
1 SMALL ONION, CHOPPED	1/2 C WHEAT GERM
4 HARD BOILED EGGS, SLICED	ANYTHING ELSE YOU LIKE

PLACE VEGETABLES IN A CASSEROLE. SPRINKLE WITH SALT, PEPPER AND WHEAT GERM. COVER WITH EGG SLICES AND GRATED CHEESE. POUR MILK OVER. COVER AND BAKE AT 350° AN HOUR. SERVE OVER COOKED RICE.

CORN OYSTERS (16 OYSTERS)

1 C SCRAPED CORN OR CANNED, CREAM-STYLE CORN	2 TSP. GRATED ONION	1/4 TSP. SALT
	6 TBLSP. FLOUR	1/8 TSP. NUTMEG
2 EGGS, BEATEN	1/2 TSP. BAKING PWD.	3 TBLSP. BUTTER

MIX EGGS AND CORN. STIR IN DRY INGREDIENTS. MELT BUTTER IN A SKILLET AND WHEN HOT, DROP IN TABLESPOONS OF BATTER. BROWN ON BOTH SIDES. SERVE WITH MUSHROOM SAUCE OR MAPLE SYRUP.

DEEP FRIED EGGPLANT
BATTER - MIX WELL 1 1/3 C FLOUR, 1 TSP. SALT, 1/4 TSP PEPPER, 1 TBLSP. OIL AND 2 BEATEN EGG YOLKS. GRADUALLY ADD 3/4 C FLAT BEER. LET BATTER REST A COUPLE HOURS. BEFORE USING, ADD 2 STIFFLY BEATEN EGG WHITES. THIS WILL COAT 2 C OF 1/2" EGGPLANT STICKS. DIP EGGPLANT IN BATTER AND DEEP FRY (OIL AT 370°) UNTIL GOLDEN. DRAIN ON PAPER TOWELING AND SALT BEFORE SERVING.

MIDDLE EAST EGGPLANT (SERVES 6-8)
SAUTÉ IN OIL TEN MINUTES } 2 MEDIUM EGGPLANT, CHOPPED, 2 STALKS CELERY, CHOPPED AND 1 LARGE ONION, CHOPPED
ADD - 1 TBLSP. FLOUR AND 6 BEATEN EGGS.
ADD - 1/2 TSP. SAFFRON, 3 TSP. RAISINS, 1 TSP. SALT, DASH PEPPER AND 1/2 C NUTMEATS.
POUR - INTO A BUTTERED CASSEROLE. TOP WITH GRATED AMERICAN CHEESE AND BAKE AT 350° FOR 30 MINUTES.

SKILLET EGGPLANT PARMESAN (SERVES 6)
1 SMALL EGGPLANT, CUT IN 1/2" SLICES   1/2 TSP. BASIL
1 - 15 OZ. JAR MEATLESS SPAGHETTI SAUCE   6 OZ. SLICED MOZZARELLA
1/2 TSP. SALT   DASH PEPPER   4 TBLSP. PARMESAN

MIX EGGPLANT, SAUCE, SALT, PEPPER AND BASIL IN A SKILLET. COVER AND SIMMER 20 MINUTES, UNTIL EGGPLANT IS TENDER, TURNING OCCASIONALLY. ARRANGE MOZZARELLA ON TOP AND SPRINKLE WITH PARMESAN. COVER AND HEAT UNTIL CHEESE MELTS.

EASY EASTERN EGGPLANT
SAUTÉ 3 CHOPPED ONIONS AND 1 EGGPLANT, CUBED IN 1/2" PIECES. ADD 1/2 C TOMATO JUICE, SALT AND PEPPER TO TASTE, 2 TBLSP. BROWN SUGAR AND CURRY PWD. TO TASTE. SIMMER UNTIL TENDER. ADD MORE JUICE IF NEEDED.

Sour Cream Noodles (SERVES 4-6)

8 OZ. (5½ - 6 C) EGG NOODLES

¼ C MELTED BUTTER	1 TBLSP. GRATED ORANGE RIND	1 C SOUR
½ C CHOPPED ALMONDS	1 TBLSP. GRATED LEMON RIND	CREAM
1 TBLSP. POPPY SEED	½ TSP. SALT	¼ TSP. PEPPER

COOK NOODLES AND DRAIN. IN A BOWL, MIX BUTTER, ALMONDS, POPPY SEED, RINDS, SALT AND PEPPER. TOSS WITH NOODLES. TURN OUT ON A HOT PLATTER AND TOP WITH DOLLOPS OF SOUR CREAM.

ONIONS ARE USED IN SO MANY DISHES AS A SEASONING, BUT WILL STAND ADMIRABLY ON THEIR OWN AS AN ACCOMPANIMENT TO MOST MEATS.

Glazed Paprika Onions (SERVES 8)

PEEL AND SLICE IN HALF CROSSWISE 4 LARGE MILD RED ONIONS (2 LB.) PLACE, CUT SIDE UP, IN A BAKING PAN. MIX ¼ TSP. SAGE, ½ TSP. EACH DRY MUSTARD AND SALT, ¾ TSP. PAPRIKA, 2 TBLSP. RED WINE VINEGAR AND 5 TBLSP. HONEY. POUR THIS OVER ONIONS. COVER PAN AND BAKE AT 350° ONE HOUR. BASTE A FEW TIMES WITH PAN SAUCE. UNCOVER AND DRIZZLE ¼ C MELTED BUTTER OVER. BAKE TEN MINUTES MORE — UNTIL GLAZED AND THE LIQUID IS EVAPORATED.

Scalloped Onions and Peanuts (SERVES 4)

3 C THIN SLICED ONIONS	½ C SOUR CREAM	¼ TSP. WORCESTERSHIRE
2 TBLSP. BUTTER	1-3 OZ. PKG. CREAM CHEESE	1 TSP. PAPRIKA
1 ½ TBLSP. FLOUR	½ TSP. SALT	½ C PEANUTS, CHOPPED
½ C MILK	2 HARD COOKED EGGS, MINCED	1 TBLSP. PARSLEY

PARBOIL ONIONS FIVE MINUTES. DRAIN. MELT BUTTER AND BLEND IN FLOUR. ADD MILK. BLEND SOUR CREAM AND CREAM CHEESE AND STIR IN, COOKING OVER LOW HEAT UNTIL THICK. ADD SEASONINGS AND EGGS. POUR ON ONIONS IN A BUTTERED CASSEROLE. SPRINKLE WITH PEANUTS AND CHOPPED PARSLEY. BAKE AT 350° FOR 30 MINUTES.

Baked Stuffed Onions (serves 8)

8 medium red onions — 1/4 c butter — 2 tblsp. parsley
1 c stuffing mix — 1/4 tsp. thyme — heavy duty foil

Peel onions and scoop out centers with a sharp knife. Finely chop centers and measure 1/4 c. Toss stuffing mix with 1/4 c onion, butter, thyme and parsley. Fill each onion with about 2 tblsp. stuffing. Wrap each onion in foil and bake at 350° for 30-45 minutes.

Onion Pie

1 - 9" baked pie crust — 3 eggs — 1/8 tsp. pepper
8 slices bacon — 1 c sour cream — 1 1/2 tsp. chives
2 c thinly sliced onions — 3/4 tsp. salt — 1/2 tsp. caraway seeds

Sauté bacon until crisp; crumble. In 3 tblsp. bacon fat, sauté onions until soft. Beat eggs slightly and stir in sour cream, salt, pepper, snipped chives, onions and bacon. Pour into baked pie shell; sprinkle with caraway seeds. Bake at 300° for 30 minutes. Let stand a few minutes.

Onions and peas are a fine combination, and mushrooms and/or sprouts. Serve onions with a cream or cheese sauce, using either American or Swiss cheese. Try the following with pork:

Onion and Apple Casserole (serves 4)

6 medium onions, peeled — 1/2 c soft bread crumbs
4 medium apples, peel and core — 3/4 c consomme
8 slices bacon, sliced — 1/2 tsp. salt

Cut onions crosswise into 1/8" slices. Cut apples the same. Sauté bacon and drain on paper toweling. In 2 tblsp. of bacon grease, toss bread crumbs. Arrange alternate layers of onions, apples and bacon in a greased baking dish. Mix consomme and salt and pour over. Top with bread crumbs. Bake at 375° for 30 minutes, covered. Uncover and bake 15 minutes longer.

PEAS — ① COOK WITH A COUPLE OF <u>LETTUCE</u> LEAVES AND A TSP. SUGAR. WHEN BARELY TENDER, SEASON WITH SALT, PEPPER AND BUTTER.

② <u>MINTED</u> — FOR 1 PKG. FROZEN PEAS, COOK AS DIRECTED, ADDING 2 TSP. MINCED ONION, 1 TSP. DRIED MINT LEAVES. DRAIN AND TOSS WITH 2 TBLSP. BUTTER.

③ COOK PEAS IN CHICKEN BROTH AND STIR IN ½ LB. FRESH <u>MUSHROOMS</u> THAT HAVE BEEN SAUTÉED IN 3 TBLSP. BUTTER. YOU MAY ALSO ADD CHOPPED <u>RED PIMIENTO</u> AND/OR 2 TBLSP. <u>SHERRY</u>.

④ SAUTÉ ⅔ C CHOPPED <u>BACON</u> AND ¼ C MINCED <u>ONION</u>. ADD 2 PKG. FROZEN PEAS, 1 TSP. SALT, A DASH OF NUTMEG AND ½ C SLIVERED <u>ALMONDS</u>. COOK ABOUT 3 MINUTES — STIR IN ½ C HEAVY <u>CREAM</u>.

POTATOES — ON "ADVENTURE" FOR <u>BAKING</u>, POTATOES ARE SCRUBBED AND PARBOILED UNTIL ¾ DONE — THEN BAKED TO BROWN THEM UP FOR THE LAST ½ HOUR. SOMETIMES THEY'RE PEELED AND WHEN PUT IN THE OVEN, ROLLED IN BUTTER AND SPRINKLED WITH SEASONED SALT. AFTER ½ HOUR, POUR INTO PAN A CAN OF CHICKEN BROTH (FOR 8 POTATOES). BAKE AND BASTE FOR ½ HOUR MORE.

<u>POTATO PANCAKES</u> (6 CAKES)

2 SLICES BACON, DICE	1 EGG, BEATEN	⅛ TSP. PEPPER
1 SMALL ONION, GRATED	2 TBLSP. FLOUR	⅛ TSP. NUTMEG
2 C GRATED POTATOES	½ TSP. SALT	2 TSP. CHOPPED PARSLEY

(SQUEEZE POTATO GRATINGS IN CHEESECLOTH TO REDUCE LIQUID)
IN LARGE SKILLET, FRY BACON UNTIL CRISP. REMOVE AND MIX WITH REMAINING INGREDIENTS. DROP BY SPOONFULLS INTO HOT BACON FAT AND COOK OVER MEDIUM HEAT UNTIL WELL BROWNED BOTH SIDES.

<u>POTATO SOUFFLÉ</u> (SERVES 4-6)

2½ C MASHED POTATOES	3 EGG YOLKS	¼ TSP. PEPPER
1 TBLSP. GRATED ONION	¾ C HEAVY CREAM	4 EGG WHITES
2 TBLSP. PARMESAN	1 TSP. SALT	

MIX ALL BUT EGG WHITES AND BEAT WELL. BEAT WHITES UNTIL STIFF AND FOLD IN. BAKE AT 350° IN A BUTTERED 1½ QT. DISH FOR 35 MINUTES OR UNTIL BROWNED AND SET.

MASHED POTATOES ARE SPECIAL WITH SOUR CREAM AND CHOPPED CHIVES FOLDED IN. EXTRA SPECIAL— GARNISH WITH CHOPPED BACON.

SCALLOPED POTATOES

IN A BUTTERED CASSEROLE, LAYER THINLY SLICED POTATOES AND ONION. SPRINKLE WITH SALT, PEPPER AND FLOUR. DOT WITH BUTTER. REPEAT LAYERS UNTIL THE CASSEROLE IS FULL. POUR MILK IN TO ALMOST COVER. (OR HALF MILK— HALF CHICKEN BROTH). BAKE AT 350° FOR AN HOUR AND 15 MINUTES. TOP WITH GRATED CHEESE AND BAKE 15 MINUTES MORE.

Sweet Potato Puff   (SERVES 8)

6 YAMS OR SWEET POTATOES   1 C CREAM   ½ TSP. CINNAMON
4 EGGS, SEPARATE   3 TBLSP. SUGAR   ¼ TSP. NUTMEG
¼ C BUTTER, MELTED   1 TBLSP. GRATED ORANGE RIND

COOK POTATOES IN BOILING, SALTED WATER UNTIL TENDER. COOL AND MASH. BEAT IN EGG YOLKS, BUTTER, CREAM, SUGAR, RIND AND SPICES. BEAT UNTIL FLUFFY. BEAT EGG WHITES UNTIL STIFF AND FOLD IN. TURN INTO A GREASED 2 QT. BAKING DISH. BAKE AT 325° FOR ONE HOUR AND TEN MINUTES, OR UNTIL PUFFED AND FIRM. GARNISH WITH ORANGE SLICES.

BRANDIED SWEET POTATOES

4 MEDIUM SWEET POTATOES   ¼ C RAISINS OR
2/3 C BROWN SUGAR   ½ C CHOPPED APPLE
¼ C WATER   ¼ C BRANDY OR
2 TBLSP. BUTTER   COGNAC

WASH POTATOES. DO NOT PEEL. BOIL IN WATER TO COVER UNTIL BARELY SOFT. DRAIN, COOL AND PEEL. SLICE INTO A GREASED CASSEROLE. BOIL SUGAR, WATER, BUTTER AND RAISINS. ADD BRANDY AND POUR OVER POTATOES. BAKE AT 350°, UNCOVERED, 30 MINUTES. BASTE NOW AND THEN.

SWEET AND SOUR SWEET POTATOES (SERVES 4)

6 MEDIUM SWEET POTATOES	MILK	
1 TBLSP. BUTTER	2 TBLSP. BUTTER	2 TBLSP. BROWN SUGAR
½ TSP. SALT	½ C GREEN PEPPER STRIPS	1 TBLSP. CORNSTARCH
⅛ TSP. PEPPER	1 DRAINED CAN (1 LB. 4 OZ.)	2 TBLSP. VINEGAR
PINCH NUTMEG	PINEAPPLE CHUNKS	¾ C PINEAPPLE JCE.

COOK AND MASH POTATOES; ADD 1 TBLSP. BUTTER, SALT, PEPPER, NUTMEG AND MILK ENOUGH TO WHIP POTATOES. IN SKILLET, SAUTÉ PEPPERS IN 2 TBLSP. BUTTER. ADD PINEAPPLE. COOK A COUPLE MINUTES. STIR IN COMBINED BROWN SUGAR AND CORNSTARCH, THEN JUICE AND VINEGAR. COOK, STIRRING, UNTIL CLEAR AND THICK. POUR MIXTURE INTO A 9" PIE PAN. DROP SPOONFULS OF POTATO ON TOP. BAKE AT 400° UNTIL BUBBLING HOT.

RICE

STEAMED RICE IS SERVED WITH FISH — PERHAPS WITH LAMB. WE LIKE TO STEAM IT IN A STOCK INSTEAD OF WATER.
VARIATIONS: HERB — MIX 3 TBLSP. CHOPPED PARSLEY, 2 TBLSP. FINE CHOPPED CHIVES, ½ TSP. TARRAGON, ½ TSP. THYME AND 2 TBLSP. BUTTER WITH 3 C COOKED RICE.

NUT — TOSS ½ C PINE NUTS OR TOASTED, SLICED ALMONDS AND 3 TBLSP. BUTTER WITH 3 C COOKED RICE. YOU CAN ADD A LITTLE GARLIC AND PARSLEY TOO.

MUSHROOMS, BACON, GREEN PEPPER, ONION, RAISINS, TOMATOES — THEY'RE ALL TASTY ADDITIONS TO A RICE DISH. TRY SEASONING WITH CURRY OR SAFFRON FOR A CHANGE.

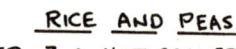

RICE AND PEAS

BUTTER 3 C HOT COOKED RICE AND TOSS WITH 3 C HOT COOKED GREEN PEAS. ADD 1 TSP. DRIED TARRAGON AND 1 TBLSP. CHOPPED PARSLEY. SPRINKLE WITH GRATED PARMESAN CHEESE.

Rice Pilaf

2 C RAW RICE	1 CAN MUSHROOMS	CAYENNE
1/4 LB. BUTTER	4 C BEEF BROTH	1/2 C CHOPPED
4 GREEN ONIONS	SALT AND PEPPER	PARSLEY

SAUTÉ RICE WELL IN BUTTER. ADD CHOPPED ONIONS AND COOK UNTIL ONION IS WILTED. ADD DRAINED MUSHROOMS. ADD BEEF BROTH (OR CONSOMME). STIR AND SEASON TO TASTE WITH SALT, PEPPER AND CAYENNE. POUR INTO A BAKING DISH. BAKE 30 MINUTES AT 400°. ADD PARSLEY, MIX AND BAKE TEN MORE MINUTES.

Curried Raisin Rice

2 1/2 C RICE	5 C CHICKEN BROTH
1 1/4 C CHOPPED ONION	1 TBLSP. SALT
3/4 C BUTTER	1 1/4 C RAISINS
1 TBLSP. CURRY PWD.	

BROWN RICE IN BUTTER WITH ONION. ADD BROTH WITH ALL SEASONINGS AND COVER. STEAM 25 MINUTES. STIR IN RAISINS.

Spanish Rice (SERVES 6)

6 SLICES BACON, CHOPPED	1 CLOVE GARLIC	1 1/2 TSP. SALT
1 C CHOPPED ONIONS	1 C RAW RICE	PEPPER
1 CHOPPED GREEN PEPPER	2 1/2 C TOMATOES	1 TBLSP. CHILI PWD.

SAUTÉ BACON AND DRAIN. IN DRIPPINGS, BROWN ONIONS, GARLIC AND GREEN PEPPER. ADD RICE AND COOK A FEW MINUTES. ADD BACON, TOMATOES AND SEASONINGS. COVER AND SIMER 20 MINUTES.

Apple Rice

SAUTÉ 2 CHOPPED ONIONS IN 2 TBLSP. BUTTER. ADD 2 C RAW RICE AND STIR FRY UNTIL GOLDEN. ADD 1 CAN CHOPPED WATER CHESTNUTS. POUR IN 4 C APPLE JUICE (HOT) AND 1 TSP. SALT. COVER AND STEAM 20 MINUTES. STIR IN 1 TBLSP. CHOPPED PARSLEY TO SERVE.

Rice Soufflé (Serves 6)

- 1 c cooked rice
- 2 tblsp. butter
- 3 tblsp. flour
- 3/4 c milk
- 1/2 lb. cheddar cheese
- 4 eggs, separated
- 1/2 tsp. salt
- cayenne

Melt butter and stir in flour. When smooth, stir in milk and cook until thick. Chop cheese into sauce and cook until it melts. Beat yolks with salt and a dash of cayenne and add slowly to sauce, stirring. Take from heat. Fold rice gently in. Beat egg whites until stiff and fold into sauce. Turn into a greased 1 1/2 qt. casserole. Bake at 325° for 40 minutes. You may add 1 c chopped, cooked broccoli or green beans to cheese-rice mixture before folding in whites.

SPINACH

If your spinach cooks down so much you're worried about having enough, add any or all of the following: mushrooms, chopped hard boiled eggs, chopped water chestnuts, cut up tomatoes or bacon bits.

Spinach Mold (Serves 4)

- 3 tblsp. butter
- 3 tblsp. flour
- 1 tsp. salt
- 1/8 tsp. pepper
- 1/8 tsp. nutmeg
- 1 c milk
- 3 eggs, separated
- 1 c cooked, chopped spinach, drained

Melt butter and add flour, salt, pepper and nutmeg. Blend until smooth. Gradually stir in milk and cook until thick. Remove from heat and add egg yolks one at a time, stirring well after each. Stir in spinach. Beat egg whites until stiff and fold in. Pour into an ungreased 1 1/2 qt. baking dish. Bake at 375° for 40 minutes. Serve right away.

Spinach Intrigue (serves 8)

1 LB FRESH SPINACH   ½ C MUSHROOMS
½ PINT SOUR CREAM   ½ C BUTTER
2 SMALL CANS TOMATO PASTE   PAPRIKA
2 TBLSP. GRATED ONION

COOK AND DRAIN SPINACH. SAUTÉ CHOPPED MUSHROOMS AND ONION IN BUTTER. PLACE SPINACH IN CASSEROLE — ADD ONIONS AND MUSHROOMS AND MIX LIGHTLY. SPREAD TOMATO PASTE ON TOP. COVER WITH SOUR CREAM. SPRINKLE WITH PAPRIKA. BAKE AT 350° — 20 MINUTES.

Spinach Tart

LINE A 9" PIE PAN WITH PASTRY AND BAKE AT 425° FOR TEN MINUTES. COOK ½ LB. FRESH SPINACH WITH 2 TBLSP. BUTTER, ½ TSP. SALT AND A DASH OF PEPPER. DRAIN WELL AND MIX WITH ½ LB. COTTAGE CHEESE, 3 EGGS (LIGHTLY BEATEN), 2 OZ. PARMESAN, ⅓ C HEAVY CREAM AND ⅛ TSP. NUTMEG. SPREAD IN SHELL AND BAKE AT 375° FOR 30 MINUTES OR UNTIL SET. IT MAY BE MADE WITHOUT THE PIE SHELL.

Stuffed Spinach (serves 6)

1 LB. FRESH SPINACH   1 C PEPPERIDGE STUFFING MIX
1 PKG. LIPTON'S ONION SOUP MIX   3 TBLSP. MELTED BUTTER
1 PINT SOUR CREAM

COOK AND DRAIN SPINACH. MIX TOGETHER ONION SOUP AND SOUR CREAM. LET STAND ½ HOUR. MELT BUTTER AND MIX WITH STUFFING MIX. COMBINE SPINACH AND SOUR CREAM MIXTURE. FOLD IN ¾ STUFFING MIX. PLACE IN A BUTTERED CASSEROLE AND TOP WITH REMAINING CRUMBS. BAKE AT 300° FOR 30 MINUTES.

SQUASH

WINTER SQUASH (ACORN, BUTTERNUT, HUBBARD) MAY BE BOILED, MASHED AND SEASONED WITH SALT, PEPPER AND BUTTER. FOLD IN SOUR CREAM AND CHIVES FOR A TREAT.
BAKED - PARBOIL ACORN SQUASH HALVES OR CHUNKS OF HUBBARD UNTIL ALMOST DONE. SCORE FLESH AND FILL CAVITIES WITH BUTTER, BROWN SUGAR (OR MAPLE SYRUP) AND SPRINKLE WITH SALT. A NICE TOUCH ON TOP IS TOASTED SLIVERED ALMONDS, CHOPPED PECANS OR SALTED PEANUTS. BAKE AT 375° UNTIL GOOD AND HOT.
SUMMER SQUASH (ZUCCHINI, CROOKED NECK, PATTYPAN) - THIN SKINNED, AND IF YOUNG, THERE'S NO NEED TO PARE OR DISCARD SEEDS. STRAIGHT OR CROOKED NECK AND ZUCCHINI ARE GOOD RAW AND WHEN COOKED, THE FLAVOR IS BEST IF COOKED ONLY UNTIL TENDER-CRISP.

GREEN AND GOLD CASSEROLE (SERVES 6)

3 MEDIUM ZUCCHINI
2 MEDIUM YELLOW SUMMER SQUASH
1 MEDIUM ONION, CHOPPED
2 TBLSP. PARSLEY
3 EGGS, BEATEN
1 C MILK
1 TSP. SALT
1/4 TSP. PEPPER
1/4 TSP. GARLIC PWD.
1/4 TSP. OREGANO
1/4 TSP. PAPRIKA
2 TBLSP. BUTTER

CUT SQUASH IN 1/4" SLICES AND PLACE IN A 1 1/2 QT. CASSEROLE. SCATTER ON ONION AND DOT WITH BUTTER. BAKE AT 400° FOR 15 MINUTES. COMBINE REMAINING INGREDIENTS EXCEPT PAPRIKA AND POUR OVER SQUASH. SPRINKLE WITH PAPRIKA. BAKE AT 350° FOR 40 MINUTES OR UNTIL SET.

FRENCH FRIED ZUCCHINI (SERVES 4)

6 SMALL ZUCCHINI
1/4 C EVAPORATED MILK
1/2 C FLOUR
SALT

CUT ZUCCHINI IN LENGTHWISE STRIPS AS FOR FRENCH FRIED POTATOES; DIP IN MILK, ROLL IN FLOUR. FRY IN DEEP FAT (375°) ABOUT 5 MINUTES UNTIL GOLDEN. DRAIN AND SPRINKLE WITH SALT.

Zucchini Loaf (serves 6)

- 2 c grated zucchini
- 1 small grated onion
- 2 eggs, beaten
- 2 c milk
- 1 c cracker crumbs
- salt and pepper
- celery salt
- 1/4 c butter
- Parmesan cheese

Mix all together except Parmesan, which is sprinkled on top. Seasonings are to taste. Place in a greased loaf pan or casserole and bake at 350° for an hour. Yellow squash or carrots may be used in place of the zucchini (or as part of the measure).

Zucchini - Tomato Layers

Cut up in a buttered casserole: a layer of squash, a layer of onion, a layer of tomatoes and one of cracker crumbs. Season with salt, pepper and basil. Dot with butter. Repeat layers. Bake at 350° for 45 minutes.

Scalloped Squash

Place barely cooked summer squash in a greased baking dish. Add a layer of grated cheese and 2 tblsp. grated onion. Pour on a medium white sauce. Top with buttered bread crumbs. Bake at 375° until brown — 25 minutes.

Zucchini Fritata (serves 4)

Sauté a small sliced onion and a minced clove garlic in 2 tblsp. olive oil until soft. Add 2 c thinly sliced zucchini and sauté 3 minutes. In a bowl, beat 6 eggs with 2 tblsp. chopped parsley and salt and pepper to taste. Add to zucchini and cook over low heat until it begins to set. Sprinkle 1/2 c Münster cheese on and drizzle tomato sauce on top. Slide in a hot oven for a few minutes until cheese melts.

Tomato Sauce — 1 can stewed tomatoes (strained). Add: 1/2 can (6 oz.) tomato paste, 1/2 tsp. salt, 1/4 tsp. basil, 1 tblsp. onion juice, 1/2 tsp. sugar. Simmer for 15 minutes.

Tomatoes

ON THE SCHOONER, OUR SUPPLY OF FRESH TOMATOES IS USED FOR SALADS AND GARNISHING. CANNED PEELED TOMATOES AND STEWED TOMATOES ARE USED IN DIFFERENT WAYS — FOR SAUCES AND IN FLAVORFUL SIDE DISHES AT DINNERTIME TO ADD COLOR AND NUTRITION.

SCALLOPED TOMATOES (SERVES 4)

SAUTÉ 1 MEDIUM CHOPPED ONION IN 1/4 C BUTTER WITH 1 MINCED CLOVE GARLIC AND 1/4 C MINCED GREEN PEPPER. TOSS IN 2 C SOFT BREAD CRUMBS. ADD 1/2 TSP. SALT, 1/8 TSP. PEPPER, 2 TBLSP. CHOPPED PARSLEY, 1/2 TSP. DRY MUSTARD, 1 TSP. SUGAR AND 1/2 TSP. OREGANO. PLACE IN A BUTTERED CASSEROLE AND POUR OVER IT 1 #2 CAN MASHED PEELED TOMATOES. SPRINKLE DRY BREAD CRUMBS ON TOP AND BAKE AT 350° FOR 30 MINUTES.

SIMPLE TOMATO STUFFING:

USE ANY PACKAGE STUFFING MIX. PLACE IN A BUTTERED CASSEROLE AND POUR CANNED PEELED TOMATOES (CHOPPED) OVER THEM. MAKE THIS MIXTURE WETTER THAN THE PACKAGE DIRECTIONS FOR LIQUID. BAKE AS ABOVE.

TOMATO-CHEESE CUSTARD (SERVES 4)

1 CAN (1 LB.) TOMATOES   1 1/2 TSP. SALT   2 EGGS, BEATEN
1 TSP. MINCED ONION   1/4 TSP. PEPPER   1/2 C AMERICAN CHEESE
1 TBLSP. BUTTER   3 SLICES CRUMBLED BREAD

HEAT FIRST 6 INGREDIENTS. COOL, ADD EGGS AND STIR. POUR INTO BUTTERED 1 QT. CASSEROLE. TOP WITH GRATED CHEESE. BAKE AT 375° - 40 MINUTES.

Tomato Quiche (Serves 6)

1 - 9" pie shell   1/4 c minced green onions
4 eggs, beaten   pepper   basil
1 c light cream   2 tblsp. minced parsley   sugar
1/2 tsp. season-all   3 medium tomatoes   salt

Bake pie shell at 425° five minutes. Mix eggs, season-all, onions, pepper and parsley. Pour into shell. Arrange tomato halves in a circle around edge of pie. Sprinkle cut surfaces of tomatoes with basil, sugar, salt and pepper. Bake at 350° for 50 minutes or until set. This may be made without the crust.

Tomato Oysters (Serves 4)

1 can (1 lb.) tomatoes   1 egg   1/2 tsp. worcestershire
1 small onion, minced   3/4 tsp. salt   dash tabasco
3/4 c soft bread crumbs   1/4 tsp. pepper   dash cayenne

Drain all liquid from tomatoes and chop pulp. Add remaining ingredients and mix well. Drop by tblsp. into hot butter in a skillet and brown slowly on both sides.

Mom's Tomato Pudding (Serves 4)

1 1/4 c tomato purée   1/4 c brown sugar   1/4 c butter,
1/4 c water   1/2 tsp. basil   melted
1/4 tsp. salt   1 c soft bread crumbs

Heat tomatoes and water to a boil and add salt, sugar and basil. Place bread crumbs in a baking dish and pour melted butter over them. Add the tomatoes, cover and bake at 375° for about 30 minutes.

Vegetable Notes

CAKES

CAKE MIXES ARE USED ABOARD SHIP FOR AN UNEXPECTED BIRTHDAY OR IF TIME BECOMES TIGHT. THERE ARE MANY THINGS THAT CAN BE DONE TO MAKE THEM SPECIAL, FROM ADDING FLAVORED JELLO, PUDDING OR DREAM WHIP TO THE BATTER, TO USING FRUITS AND NUTS. SEE "MARLIN SPIKE CAKE" BELOW. THE GOODIE BOX OVER THE CHOPPING BLOCK IS KEPT STOCKED WITH BIRTHDAY CANDLES, FOOD DYES, AND ICING TIPS SO WE CAN HELP ANYONE CELEBRATE ANYTHING. BAKING CAKES FROM SCRATCH IS BEST. HERE ARE A FEW FAVORITES:

MARLIN SPIKE CAKE

- 3/4 C COLD WATER
- 1 - 3 OZ. PKG. LEMON JELLO
- 4 EGGS, BEATEN
- 1 PKG. YELLOW CAKE MIX
- 3/4 C SALAD OIL
- GRATED RIND 1 LEMON
- 2 C CONFECTIONERS' SUGAR
- JUICE OF 2 LEMONS

MIX COLD WATER WITH GELATIN. ADD EGGS, CAKE MIX, GRATED RIND AND OIL AND BEAT. POUR INTO A GREASED AND FLOURED 9 x 13" PAN AND BAKE AT 350° ABOUT 35 MINUTES OR UNTIL DONE. WHILE WARM, PUNCH HOLES ALL OVER CAKE (ABOUT 2" APART) WITH A MARLIN SPIKE. MIX LEMON JUICE AND CONFECTIONERS' SUGAR AND DRIZZLE OVER CAKE.

HUNDRED DOLLAR CAKE

- 2 C FLOUR
- 1 C SUGAR
- 4 TBLSP. UNSWEET COCOA
- 2 TSP. BAKING SODA
- 1 C COLD WATER
- 1 C MAYONNAISE
- 1 TSP VANILLA

PLACE ALL INGREDIENTS IN A BOWL AND BEAT WELL. BAKE AT 350° IN A GREASED, FLOURED 9" SQUARE PAN FOR ABOUT 30 MINUTES. TOP WITH "BOILED WHITE FROSTING". ⟶

Boiled White Frosting

Bring 1 c sugar and 1/3 c water to a boil. Simmer until it spins a thread. Beat one egg white until stiff and slowly pour sugar syrup in, beating as you pour. This is enough for one layer cake.

Hot Milk Sponge Cake

2 eggs   1 c flour   1 tsp. baking pwd.
1 c sugar   1/8 tsp. salt   1/2 c boiling milk

Beat eggs three minutes. Add sugar and beat two minutes. Stir in boiling milk. Sift flour, salt and baking pwd. and fold in gently. Pour into a greased 9" square pan and bake at 325° for 30 minutes or until done.

Lazy Topping: Mix in a saucepan — 3 tblsp. butter, 5 tblsp. brown sugar, 2 tblsp. cream and 1/2 c shredded coconut. Heat until butter melts. Spread on warm cake and broil until topping bubbles.

Pound Cake

Sift: 4 c flour, 1 tsp. salt, 1/2 tsp. mace, 4 tsp. baking pwd.
Cream well: 1 1/2 c butter and 3 c sugar
Add: 1 at a time, beating well after each — 8 eggs
Add: Flour mix alternately with 1 c milk, 2 tsp. vanilla and 2 tblsp. brandy
Stir: Only until well blended.
Bake: In two greased 9 x 9" bread pans (lined with oiled brown paper) at 325° – 1 hr.
Seed Cake: Same recipe as above, but add 2 tsp. caraway seed, 1/3 c shaved citron and 1 tsp. grated lemon rind.

PINEAPPLE UPSIDE DOWN CAKE

1 C BROWN SUGAR	3 EGGS
½ C BUTTER	1½ TSP VANILLA
1 - 20 OZ. CAN PINEAPPLE SLICES, DRAINED	2½ C FLOUR
MARASCHINO CHERRIES	2½ TSP. BAKING PWD.
1 C GRANULATED SUGAR	½ TSP. SALT
⅔ C SHORTENING	1 C MILK

IN RECTANGULAR BAKING PAN, MIX BROWN SUGAR AND BUTTER. COOK AND STIR OVER LOW HEAT UNTIL MIXTURE BUBBLES. REMOVE FROM HEAT AND ARRANGE PINEAPPLE SLICES AND CHERRIES IN THE SUGAR MIX. IN A BOWL, CREAM SHORTENING AND SUGAR UNTIL LIGHT. ADD EGGS ONE AT A TIME, BEATING WELL. ADD VANILLA. SIFT DRY INGREDIENTS AND ADD TO CREAMED MIX ALTERNATELY WITH MILK.

POUR BATTER OVER FRUIT AND BAKE AT 350° FOR ABOUT 45 MINUTES. OTHER KINDS OF FRUIT CAN BE SUBSTITUTED FOR PINEAPPLE.

ALMOND CAKE (MAKES 30 PIECES)

6 EGGS, SEPARATE	2 C GROUND BLANCHED ALMONDS
1 C SUGAR	⅛ TSP. SALT
½ C FLOUR	⅛ TSP. CREAM OF TARTER
1 TSP. BAKING PWD.	1 TSP. GRATED LEMON PEEL
¼ TSP. ALMOND EXT.	LEMON SYRUP

BEAT YOLKS UNTIL LIGHT. GRADUALLY BEAT IN ½ C SUGAR UNTIL THICK AND LEMON-COLORED. SIFT FLOUR WITH BAKING PWD. AND STIR IN. ADD ALMOND EXT. AND HALF OF ALMONDS. MIX ONLY UNTIL WELL DISTRIBUTED. BEAT WHITES FOAMY. ADD SALT AND CREAM OF TARTER AND BEAT UNTIL STIFF, ADDING OTHER ½ C SUGAR. FOLD IN PEEL AND REST OF ALMONDS. GENTLY FOLD YOLK MIX INTO WHITES. BAKE AT 350° IN A BUTTERED 9 X 13" PAN FOR 30 MINUTES. COOL 10 MINUTES. TURN OUT - CUT IN DIAMOND WEDGES AND TOP WITH HOT

LEMON SYRUP: MIX IN A SAUCEPAN ¾ C SUGAR, 3 TBLSP. LEMON JUICE AND ¼ C WATER. BOIL AND STIR UNTIL SUGAR DISSOLVES.

APPLECAKE

¼ C MELTED BUTTER	1 C FLOUR	½ TSP. NUTMEG
1 C SUGAR	1 TSP. BAKING SODA	3 C GRATED APPLE
1 EGG, BEATEN	¼ TSP. SALT	¾ C NUTMEATS (OPT.)
1 TSP. VANILLA	½ TSP. CINNAMON	

CREAM BUTTER AND SUGAR AND BLEND IN EGG AND VANILLA. SIFT DRY INGREDIENTS AND STIR IN. FOLD IN APPLES AND NUTS. POUR INTO A GREASED 9" OVEN DISH. BAKE AT 375° ABOUT 30 MINUTES. SERVE HOT OR COLD WITH LEMON SAUCE OR WHIPPED CREAM.

APPLESAUCE SPICE CAKE

½ C BUTTER	2½ C FLOUR	½ TSP. ALLSPICE
2 C SUGAR	½ TSP. SALT	1 C CHOPPED RAISINS
1 EGG	½ TSP. CINNAMON	½ C CHOPPED NUTS
1½ C APPLESAUCE	½ TSP. CLOVES	2 TSP. BAKING SODA
		½ C BOILING WATER

CREAM BUTTER AND SUGAR. STIR IN EGG AND APPLESAUCE. SIFT DRY INGREDIENTS AND ADD ALTERNATELY WITH BOILING WATER (IN WHICH THE SODA HAS BEEN DISSOLVED). STIR IN RAISINS AND NUTS. BAKE IN A GREASED 9 X 13" PAN AT 350° FOR 30-45 MINUTES.

BLUEBERRY PUDDING CAKE

2 C BLUEBERRIES	½ TSP. NUTMEG	1 TSP. VANILLA
2 TBLSP. LEMON JUICE	¾ C SUGAR	1 C SUGAR
1 C FLOUR	½ C MILK	1 TBLSP. CORNSTARCH
2 TSP. BAKING PWD.	1 EGG	1 C BOILING WATER
¼ TSP. SALT	¼ C MELTED BUTTER	

PLACE BLUEBERRIES AND LEMON JUICE IN AN 8 X 8" PAN. MIX FLOUR, BAKING PWD., SALT, NUTMEG AND ¾ C SUGAR. BEAT IN MILK, EGG, MELTED BUTTER AND VANILLA. SPREAD OVER BERRIES. MIX 1 C SUGAR WITH CORNSTARCH AND SPRINKLE OVER BATTER. POUR BOILING WATER OVER ALL. BAKE AT 350° FOR 40-45 MINUTES. (OTHER FRUITS MAY BE USED IN PLACE OF THE BLUEBERRIES)

CARROT-NUT CAKE

3 C FLOUR
2 TSP. BAKING PWD.
2 TSP. SODA
3/4 TSP. SALT
} PLACE IN A BOWL AND MAKE A WELL IN THE CENTER.

ADD: 4 BEATEN EGGS, 1 1/2 C SALAD OIL AND 2 C SUGAR. BEAT.
ADD: 2 C GRATED CARROT   1/2 C RAISINS (FLOURED)
     1 C CHOPPED PECANS 2 TSP. CINNAMON
POUR: INTO A BUTTERED 9 X 13" PAN AND BAKE AT 325° ONE HOUR. SPRINKLE WITH PWD. SUGAR TO SERVE.

GINGERBREAD

1/2 C BUTTER   1 TSP. CINNAMON   JUICE 1 ORANGE
1/2 C SUGAR   1 TSP. NUTMEG   RIND 1 ORANGE
1 C MOLASSES   1/3 C BRANDY (OR COFFEE) 1 TSP. SODA
1/2 C MILK   3 EGGS, BEATEN   2 TBLSP. WARM WATER
1 TBLSP. GINGER 3 C FLOUR   1 C RAISINS

CREAM BUTTER AND SUGAR. ADD MOLASSES, MILK, SPICES AND BRANDY OR COFFEE. ADD FLOUR AND EGGS ALTERNATELY TO BATTER. STIR IN JUICE AND RIND. DISSOLVE SODA IN WARM WATER AND ADD. BEAT UNTIL LIGHT. FOLD IN RAISINS. BAKE AT 350° IN A GREASED 9 X 13" PAN FOR ONE HOUR. SERVE WITH WHIPPED CREAM OR LEMON SAUCE.

FRUIT COCKTAIL CAKE

2 EGGS   1 1/2 C SUGAR   2 C FLOUR
2 C FRUIT COCKTAIL 2 TSP. BAKING SODA 1 TSP. SALT

MIX ALL TOGETHER AND POUR INTO A GREASED AND FLOURED 9 X 13" PAN. SPRINKLE 1/2 C BROWN SUGAR AND 1/2 C CHOPPED NUTS ON TOP. BAKE AT 350° FOR 30-40 MINUTES. FROST WITH: 1/2 C BUTTER, 1/2 C CANNED MILK OR CREAM AND 3/4 C WHITE SUGAR (HEAT TOGETHER AND POUR OVER WARM CAKE).

CHOCOLATE CAKE

3 SQUARES BITTER CHOCOLATE	3/4 C MILK
2 C FLOUR	3/4 TSP. BAKING PWD.
2 C SUGAR	1/2 C MILK
1 TSP. SALT	3 EGGS, UNBEATEN
1 1/2 TSP. BAKING SODA	1 TSP. VANILLA
1/2 C SHORTENING	

PLACE MELTED CHOCOLATE AND NEXT SIX INGREDIENTS IN A BOWL. BEAT 300 STROKES. STIR IN BAKING PWD; ADD NEXT THREE INGREDIENTS. BEAT 300 STROKES. POUR INTO A GREASED AND FLOURED 9 x 13" PAN (OR TWO 9" LAYER CAKE PANS). BAKE AT 350° FOR 30-45 MINUTES.

CHOCOLATE FROSTING

MIX 1 1/4 C SUGAR, AND 1 C EVAPORATED MILK IN A PAN. BRING TO A BOIL AND SIMMER 6 MINUTES. REMOVE FROM FIRE AND ADD 5 SQUARES BITTER CHOCOLATE. BLEND. STIR IN 1/2 C BUTTER AND 1 TSP. VANILLA. BEAT TILL THICK.

QUICK LEMON SAUCE (1 3/4 C)

MIX 1/2 C SUGAR, 1/8 TSP. SALT, AND 2 TBLSP. CORNSTARCH IN A SAUCEPAN. GRADUALLY STIR IN 1 C BOILING WATER. COOK UNTIL THICK AND CLEAR. REMOVE FROM HEAT AND STIR IN 2 TBLSP. BUTTER AND THE JUICE AND GRATINGS OF 1 LEMON. — GOOD ON APPLECAKE AND GINGERBREAD.

PUDDING OR CAKE SAUCE

HEAT 1/4 C MILK IN THE TOP OF A DOUBLE BOILER. STIR IN 1 C SUGAR AND 2 BEATEN EGG YOLKS. STIR AND COOK UNTIL THICK. REMOVE FROM FIRE AND COOL. FOLD IN STIFFLY BEATEN EGG WHITES AND FLAVOR SAUCE WITH VANILLA, BRANDY OR RUM.

CAKE NOTES

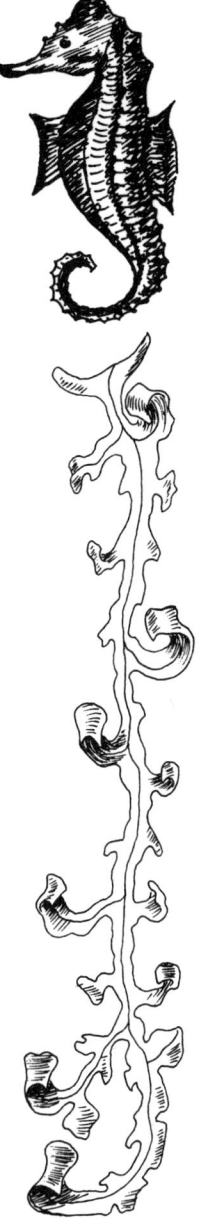

COOKIES

SCOTCH SHORTBREAD

BEAT: 1 C BUTTER WITH 1 C SIFTED CONFECTIONERS' SUGAR. WHEN LIGHT AND CREAMY, BEAT IN: 2 EGGS AND ¼ C SOUR CREAM. SIFT AND STIR IN: 2½ C FLOUR, 1 TSP. BAKING PWD. YOU MAY ADD 1 TSP. GRATED LEMON RIND. PRESS DOUGH INTO FOUR 8" ROUNDS. FLUTE THE EDGES AND PRICK DOUGH WELL. THE TOPS MAY BE SPRINKLED WITH CHOPPED, BLANCHED ALMONDS. BAKE AT 325° ABOUT 20 MINUTES UNTIL LIGHTLY BROWNED. CUT IN WEDGES WHILE STILL WARM.

CINNAMON CRUNCH

1 C FLOUR	½ C SUGAR	1 EGG WHITE
¼ TSP. SALT	1 EGG YOLK	¼ C SUGAR
½ TSP. CINNAMON	2 TBLSP. MILK	¼ TSP. CINNAMON
⅓ C BUTTER	½ TSP. VANILLA	¼ C CHOPPED NUTS

SIFT FLOUR, SALT AND CINNAMON. CREAM BUTTER AND SUGAR. STIR IN FLOUR MIX. BEAT YOLK, MILK AND VANILLA AND ADD. SPREAD IN A BUTTERED 9 X 9" PAN. BEAT EGG WHITE SLIGHTLY AND BRUSH ON DOUGH. MIX SUGAR, CINNAMON AND NUTS. SPRINKLE ON DOUGH. BAKE AT 350° FOR 30 MINUTES. CUT IN SQUARES WHILE WARM. COOL IN PAN.

SWEDISH SPICE COOKIES

1 C BUTTER	2 TSP. BAKING SODA	1½ TBLSP. GRATED ORANGE RIND
1½ C SUGAR	1 TBLSP. WARM WATER	
2 TSP. DARK SYRUP	3 C FLOUR	2 TSP. CINNAMON
1 EGG	1 TSP. GINGER	½ TSP. CLOVES

CREAM BUTTER AND SUGAR. STIR IN SYRUP AND EGG. ADD SODA DISSOLVED IN WARM WATER. ADD THE REST OF THE INGREDIENTS. FORM INTO A ROLL AND CHILL. SLICE AND BAKE ON AN UNGREASED COOKIE SHEET AT 400° FOR 5 TO 10 MINUTES.

OATMEAL COOKIES

3/4 C SHORTENING	1 EGG	1 C FLOUR
1 C BROWN SUGAR	1/4 C WATER	1 TSP. SALT
1/2 C GRANULATED SUGAR	1 TSP. VANILLA	1/2 TSP. BAKING SODA
		3 C REGULAR OATS

BEAT SHORTENING, SUGARS, EGG, WATER AND VANILLA UNTIL CREAMY. SIFT TOGETHER FLOUR, SALT AND SODA. ADD TO CREAMED MIX. BLEND WELL AND STIR IN OATS. DROP BY TSP. ON A GREASED COOKIE SHEET. BAKE AT 350° FOR 10-15 MINUTES. (FOR VARIETY, YOU MAY ADD CHOPPED NUTS, RAISINS, CHOCOLATE CHIPS OR COCONUT.

PEANUT-BUTTER COOKIES

2 1/2 C FLOUR	1 C WHITE SUGAR	1/2 TSP. SALT
1 TSP. BAKING PWD.	2 EGGS	1 C PEANUT-BUTTER
1 C BUTTER	2 TSP. BAKING SODA	1 C BROWN SUGAR
		1 TSP. VANILLA

CREAM BUTTER AND PEANUT-BUTTER. ADD SUGARS, THEN EGGS. SIFT DRY INGREDIENTS AND MIX IN. ADD VANILLA. CHILL DOUGH. FORM INTO BALLS AND PUT ON GREASED BAKING SHEET. FLATTEN BALLS WITH A FLOURED FORK. BAKE AT 375° 10-15 MINUTES.

MOLASSES COOKIES

3/4 C BUTTER	1/4 C MOLASSES	1 TSP. CINNAMON
1 C SUGAR	2 C FLOUR	1 TSP. GINGER
1 EGG	2 TSP. BAKING SODA	1 TSP. PWD. CLOVES
		1/2 TSP. SALT

MIX ALL TOGETHER AND CHILL. MAKE INTO WALNUT SIZE BALLS. ROLL IN GRANULATED SUGAR AND BAKE AT 350° FOR 10-12 MINUTES

GRANOLA COOKIES

3/4 C SHORTENING	1 TSP. VANILLA	1 TSP. CINNAMON
1 C BROWN SUGAR	3 C GRANOLA	1/2 TSP. BAKING SODA
1/2 C GRANULATED SUGAR	(CRUSH SLIGHTLY)	1/2 TSP. PWD. CLOVES
1 EGG	1 1/4 C FLOUR	1 C RAISINS
1/4 C WATER	1 TSP. SALT	1 C NUTMEATS (OPT.)

MIX ALL INGREDIENTS TOGETHER. DROP BY TSP. ON AN UNGREASED BAKING SHEET. BAKE AT 350° FOR 10-15 MINUTES.

SEVEN LAYER BARS

¼ C BUTTER
1 C GRAHAM CRACKER CRUMBS
1 C SHREDDED COCONUT
1 PKG. (6 OZ.) CHOCOLATE CHIPS
1 PKG. (6 OZ.) BUTTERSCOTCH CHIPS
1 CAN SWEETENED CONDENSED MILK
1 C CHOPPED NUTS

MELT BUTTER IN A 13 x 9" PAN. SPRINKLE GRAHAM CRUMBS EVENLY OVER BUTTER. PRESS DOWN. SPRINKLE ON COCONUT, THEN CHOCOLATE CHIPS AND BUTTERSCOTCH CHIPS. POUR MILK EVENLY OVER ALL. SPRINKLE NUTS ON TOP. BAKE AT 350° FOR 30 MINUTES. CUT IN 1 x 2" BARS.

BUTTERSCOTCH FRUIT BARS

½ TSP. BAKING PWD.
⅓ C FLOUR
⅓ C WHEAT GERM
⅞ C BROWN SUGAR
½ C PWD. MILK
¼ TSP. SALT
½ CUBE MELTED BUTTER
1 TBLSP. MOLASSES
2 EGGS
1 TSP. VANILLA
1 TSP. ALMOND EXT.
½ C CHOPPED DATES
4 EACH CHOPPED DRIED FIGS AND APRICOTS
½ C CHOPPED NUTS

MELT BUTTER - ADD SUGAR AND STIR. ADD EVERYTHING ELSE WITH FRUIT AND NUTS LAST. LINE 8 x 8" PAN WITH ALUMINUM FOIL. BAKE AT 350° ABOUT 30 MINUTES. CUT INTO BARS WHILE WARM.

BROWNIES

2 SQUARES BITTER CHOCOLATE
⅓ C BUTTER
½ TSP. BAKING PWD.
¾ C FLOUR
¼ TSP. SALT
2 EGGS
1 C SUGAR
1 TSP. VANILLA
½ C CHOPPED NUTS

BEAT EGGS WELL. BEAT IN SUGAR. MELT CHOCOLATE AND BUTTER AND ADD. BLEND IN VANILLA. SIFT FLOUR, BAKING PWD. AND SALT AND STIR INTO CHOCOLATE MIX. ADD NUTS. BAKE AT 350° IN A GREASED 8 x 8" SQUARE PAN FOR 25 MINUTES. CUT INTO 20 PIECES.

CHEWY CARAMEL BROWNIES

1 C FLOUR
2 C LT. BROWN SUGAR
1 C CHOPPED NUTS
½ C SHORTENING
2 EGGS
¾ TSP. SALT
2 TSP. VANILLA
2 TSP. BAKING PWD.

BEAT ALL TOGETHER WELL. BAKE IN A GREASED COOKIE SHEET AT 350° FOR 25 MINUTES. COOL 15 MINUTES. CUT.

MOM'S CHOCOLATE COOKIES

2/3 c BUTTER
1 1/2 c SUGAR
2 EGGS
3/4 c MILK
3/4 c BITTER COCOA
3 TSP. BAKING PWD.
2 1/2 c FLOUR
1 c CHOPPED NUTS
3/4 TSP. SALT
1 1/2 TSP. VANILLA

CREAM BUTTER AND SUGAR. ADD EGGS AND MILK. SIFT COCOA WITH REST OF DRY INGREDIENTS. STIR INTO BATTER. ADD NUTS AND VANILLA. DROP BY TSP. ON GREASED COOKIE SHEET. BAKE AT 400° ABOUT TEN MINUTES. COOL AND FROST WITH: 2 TBLSP. MELTED BUTTER, 1/4 c COCOA, 4 TBLSP. HOT WATER AND 1 TSP. VANILLA. USE ENOUGH PWD. SUGAR TO THICKEN. (MIX OVER HOT WATER).

COOKIE NOTES

MISCELLANEOUS DESSERTS

PUDDINGS, PUDDINGS, PUDDINGS

So many things may be done with instant or cooked pudding mixes. They're a blessing. Use your imagination to enhance them. After your pudding is prepared, fold in whipped cream, Dream or Cool Whip, or try some of the following additions:

VANILLA
1. Mandarin oranges with grated orange peel.
2. Drained crushed pineapple (try flavoring it mint).
3. Layer with canned pie filling - top with toasted almonds.
4. Soak dried dates and/or figs in orange juice and stir in with chopped walnuts.
5. Fold in bananas - season with sherry, rum or brandy.
6. Fold in shaved chocolate or chocolate chips.
7. Layer or ribbon with ice cream sauces.
8. Decorate with coconut, crushed granola, chopped nuts, nutmeg, cherries, shaved chocolate - whatever!

BUTTERSCOTCH
1. Fold in crushed peanut brittle
2. Chocolate chips and/or nuts or coconut
3. Dissolve strong instant coffee and add when mixing.
4. Praline - sprinkle chopped peanuts on top.

CHOCOLATE
1. Fold in bananas and whipped cream.
2. Fold in crushed peppermint candy.
3. Fold in chopped nuts, coconut or miniature marshmallows.

Cooked pie shells may be filled with any pudding combination.

MAINE CRAZY PUDDING

1 1/4 C SUGAR
5 TBLSP. BUTTER } CREAM TOGETHER

ADD: 2 1/2 C FLOUR
2 1/2 TSP. BAKING PWD.   1 1/4 TSP. SALT
2 1/2 TSP. BAKING SODA   1 1/4 TSP. NUTMEG
ALTERNATELY WITH 1 1/4 C MILK. ADD 1 C RAISINS OR DATES

SAUCE: 2 1/2 C BROWN SUGAR
5 TBLSP. BUTTER
5 C BOILING WATER AND 5 TBLSP. LEMON JUICE. POUR OVER PUDDING IN A LARGE RECTANGULAR PAN (GREASED). BAKE AT 375° - 1 HOUR. SERVE WARM WITH WHIPPED CREAM.

FLUFFY BREAD PUDDING

SOAK FOR 15 MINUTES: 4 C DICED FRESH BREAD (3 1/2 IF STALE) OR CAKE — IN 3 C WARM MILK (OR 2 C MILK AND 1 C FRUIT JUICE) AND 1/4 TSP. SALT.

COMBINE AND BEAT WELL: 3 EGG YOLKS 1/2 C SUGAR, 1 TSP. VANILLA AND 1/2 TSP. NUTMEG.

ADD: GRATED RIND AND JUICE 1/2 LEMON (1/4 C RAISINS, DATES OR NUTS OR 1/2 C DRAINED CRUSHED PINEAPPLE OR 1/4 C ORANGE MARMALADE.)

POUR: THESE INGREDIENTS OVER SOAKED BREAD. STIR LIGHTLY UNTIL BLENDED.

BEAT: 3 EGG WHITES UNTIL STIFF AND FOLD IN.

BAKE IN A BUTTERED DISH SET IN A PAN OF HOT WATER — ABOUT 45 MINUTES AT 350°.

TOP WITH CREAM OR DABS OF A TART JELLY, OR BOTH.

SURPRISE APPLESAUCE PUDDING

2 C GRAHAM CRACKER CRUMBS
2 TBLSP. MELTED BUTTER
½ TSP. CINNAMON OR NUTMEG
2 C APPLESAUCE
DASH SALT
3 EGGS, SEPARATE
1-15 OZ. CAN SWEETENED CONDENSED MILK
2 TBLSP. LEMON JUICE
GRATES 1 LEMON

MIX CRUMBS, BUTTER AND CINNAMON; SPREAD HALF IN A GREASED 8" SQUARE PAN. BEAT EGG YOLKS WELL; ADD MILK, LEMON JUICE, RIND, SALT AND APPLESAUCE; FOLD IN STIFFLY BEATEN EGG WHITES. POUR MIX IN PAN AND TOP WITH REST OF CRUMBS. BAKE AT 350° FOR 50 MINUTES. SERVE WARM OR COLD TOPPED WITH WHIPPED CREAM.

CRUNCH PUFF PUDDING

¼ C BUTTER
½ C SUGAR
2 EGGS, SEPARATE
1 TSP. GRATED LEMON RIND
3 TBLSP. LEMON JUICE
2 TBLSP. FLOUR
¼ C NON FAT DRY MILK
¼ C GRAPENUTS   1 C FLUID MILK

CREAM BUTTER WITH SUGAR. ADD EGG YOLKS AND BEAT WELL. ADD LEMON RIND AND JUICE. STIR IN FLOUR, DRY MILK, GRAPE-NUTS AND FLUID MILK. BEAT WHITES UNTIL STIFF AND FOLD INTO GRAPENUTS MIX. TURN INTO A GREASED 1½ QT. CASSEROLE. PLACE IN PAN OF HOT WATER. BAKE AT 325° FOR ONE HOUR AND 15 MINUTES. SERVE WARM OR COLD, WITH WHIPPED CREAM.

LEMON SOUFFLÉ

1 C SUGAR
4 TBLSP. FLOUR
⅛ TSP. SALT
2 TBLSP. MELTED BUTTER
3 STIFFLY BEATEN EGG WHITES
5 TBLSP. LEMON JUICE
GRATES 1 LEMON
½ C MILK
3 BEATEN YOLKS

BLEND SUGAR, FLOUR, SALT, BUTTER, LEMON JUICE, RIND, YOLKS AND MILK. FOLD IN WHITES. POUR INTO A WELL-GREASED BAKING DISH. PLACE IN A PAN OF HOT WATER. BAKE AT 350° FOR 1 HOUR. SERVE WITH WHIPPED CREAM.

FRUIT CRISP

SLICE 1 QUART OF APPLES, PEACHES, PEARS (OR OTHER FRUIT) INTO A 9" PAN. SPRINKLE WITH CINNAMON SUGAR AND LEMON JUICE. BLEND TOGETHER: 1 C BROWN SUGAR, 1 C FLOUR, 1 TSP. BAKING PWD., 1 EGG

PAT THIS MIXTURE LIGHTLY ON THE FRUIT. MELT 1/3 C BUTTER AND POUR OVER ALL. BAKE AT 350° FOR 30 MINUTES UNTIL GOLDEN BROWN. SERVE WITH WHIPPED CREAM — WARM OR COOL. NUTS MAY BE ADDED TO THE FLOUR MIX IF YOU WISH.

EASY COBBLER

PLACE ONE QUART OF FRUIT IN A CASSEROLE AND SPRINKLE WITH 2 TBLSP. FLOUR (3 TBLSP IF USING BERRIES), 1 1/2 TSP. SALT, 1/2 C CORN SYRUP, HONEY OR TABLE SYRUP AND 2 TSP. LEMON JUICE. MIX: 1 1/2 C BISQUICK, 3 TBLSP. SUGAR AND 2 TBLSP. BUTTER (CUT IN). STIR IN 1/2 C MILK. TURN OUT ON FLOURED WAX PAPER AND ROLL TO THE SAME SHAPE AS THE CASSEROLE. TURN DOUGH ONTO THE FRUIT AND SPRINKLE WITH CINNAMON SUGAR. BAKE AT 400° FOR 20 MINUTES. SERVE WARM OR COLD WITH CREAM.

CHERRY SOG

1 GRAHAM CRACKER PIE CRUST	1/3 C LEMON JUICE
1 CAN SWEETENED CONDENSED MILK	1 TSP. VANILLA
1 - 8 OZ. PKG CREAM CHEESE	1 CAN CHERRY PIE FILLING

BEAT CREAM CHEESE AND MILK TOGETHER UNTIL SMOOTH. MIX IN LEMON JUICE AND VANILLA. POUR INTO GRAHAM CRUST THAT HAS BEEN SHAPED IN A 9" PIE PAN. CHILL AND COVER WITH CHERRIES BEFORE SERVING. BLUEBERRY PIE FILLING IS GOOD TOO.

Rice Pudding

2 c cooked rice	1 tsp. vanilla
1 1/3 c milk	4 eggs
1/8 tsp. salt	1/2 tsp. grated lemon rind
1/2 c brown sugar	1 tsp. lemon juice
1 tblsp. soft butter	1/3 c raisins or dates

Combine and beat milk, salt, brown sugar, butter, vanilla and eggs. Add to rice with lemon juice and rind and raisins or dates. Place in a buttered casserole and bake at 325° about 50 minutes. Serve with a fruit sauce or whipped cream.

or

Rice Cream

2 c cooked rice	1/3 c sugar
1 c milk	1 tsp. vanilla

Mix rice, milk, sugar and vanilla. Fold in to this enough whipped cream to make the right consistency. Serve with a fruit sauce (cherry, flavored with cherry herring) - 1/4 c slivered almonds folded in or as a garnish. You may use instant vanilla pudding and fold in cooked rice and whipped cream to your liking. As a topping you might like to use berries.

Baked Coffee Soufflé

2 tblsp. butter	2 tblsp. instant coffee	
2 tblsp. flour	3/4 c water	1/2 c sugar
1/4 tsp. salt	3 eggs, separate	1/2 tsp. vanilla

Melt butter. Add flour, salt, coffee, and water. Stir and cook until thick and smooth. Remove from heat. Beat yolks until light; add sugar gradually, beating well. Stir in coffee mix and vanilla. Beat egg whites stiff and fold into coffee mixture. Pour into a greased 1 qt. casserole. Place in a pan of hot water and bake at 350° - 50 minutes. Serve with cream.

INDIAN PUDDING (SERVES 8)

4 C MILK	1 TSP. CINNAMON	1/2 TSP. SALT
3/4 C YELLOW CORNMEAL	1/2 TSP. NUTMEG	4 BEATEN EGGS
1/4 C MOLASSES	1 C LIGHT BROWN SUGAR	1 C SOUR CREAM
1 TSP. GINGER	1/2 C MELTED BUTTER	HEAVY CREAM

HEAT 3 C MILK IN TOP OF A DOUBLE BOILER. MIX THE OTHER 1 C MILK WITH THE CORNMEAL. ADD TO HOT MILK AND STIR AND COOK UNTIL SLIGHTLY THICK (5 MINUTES). REMOVE FROM HEAT. MIX MOLASSES WITH SPICES AND STIR INTO CORNMEAL MIXTURE. ADD BROWN SUGAR, BUTTER, SALT, EGGS AND SOUR CREAM. BLEND. BAKE IN A 2 QUART BUTTERED DISH AT 275° FOR 2 HOURS OR UNTIL A KNIFE INSERTED IN THE CENTER COMES OUT CLEAN. SERVE WARM WITH CREAM.

CHOCOLATE SAUCE #1 (MAKES 1 C)

MELT 2 SQUARES OF BITTER CHOCOLATE IN SIX TBLSP. WATER OVER LOW HEAT, STIRRING UNTIL SMOOTH. ADD 1/2 C SUGAR AND A DASH OF SALT. COOK AND STIR UNTIL SMOOTH AND SLIGHTLY THICK. STIR IN 3 TBLSP. BUTTER AND 1/2 TSP. VANILLA. COOL.

CHOCOLATE SAUCE #2

MELT 2 SQUARES BITTER CHOCOLATE IN 1 C LIGHT CORN SYRUP OVER LOW HEAT. REMOVE FROM HEAT AND STIR IN 1/2 TSP. VANILLA AND 1 TBLSP. BUTTER.

BUTTERSCOTCH SAUCE

BOIL TO THE CONSISTENCY OF HEAVY SYRUP: 1/3 C WHITE CORN SYRUP, 3/4 C PACKED BROWN SUGAR, 2 TBLSP. BUTTER AND 1/8 TSP. SALT. COOL AND ADD 1/3 C EVAPORATED MILK OR LIGHT CREAM. BEAT. SERVE WARM OR COLD.

Yogurt

3 c nonfat pwd. milk   1 tall can evaporated milk
6 c boiling water   3 tblsp. plain yogurt

Add boiling water to pwd. milk and beat with a whisk. Add evaporated milk. Cool mixture to 110° to 120° (same temperature as a baby's bottle). Add 3 tblsp. plain yogurt and mix well. Cover and wrap in a blanket to hold the heat. Let sit five hours without looking. Refrigerate.

Adventure Ice Cream

1½ c sugar   3 c heavy cream
5 eggs, beaten   2 c whole milk
2 tsp. vanilla   1 c evaporated milk

Mix all together and fill freezer can ⅔ full. This makes enough for ten people.

Cheesecake

Separate 3 eggs and beat the yolks with 12 oz. cream cheese and 1 tsp. vanilla. Beat the whites stiff, gradually adding ¾ c sugar. Fold whites into the cream cheese mix. Pour into a 9" pie pan lined with a graham cracker crust. Bake at 350° for ½ hour. Turn off heat and allow to cool in oven. **Topping:** Mix ½ pint sour cream with 2 tblsp. sugar and ¼ tsp. vanilla. Spread on cheesecake and bake again at 350° for ten minutes.

Helen's Pumpkin Cheesecake (Oven 325°)

- 1/4 c graham cracker crumbs
- 4 pkg. (8 oz.) softened cream cheese
- 1 1/2 c sugar
- 5 large eggs
- 1/4 tsp. salt
- 1/4 c flour
- 1 can (1 lb.) pumpkin
- 1 tsp. cinnamon
- 1/2 tsp. nutmeg
- 1/4 tsp. cloves
- 1/4 tsp. ginger

Butter a 9" spring form pan generously. Sprinkle with graham crumbs — shake to coat all sides. Beat cheese until fluffy. Gradually beat in sugar. Add eggs, one at a time, mixing well after each. Stir in flour, pumpkin, salt & spices. Pour into prepared pan. Bake 1 1/2 hour or until firm around sides, but soft in the center. Turn off heat. Open oven door and let cake cool in oven thirty minutes. Remove from oven and cool completely on rack. Chill. The flavor improves the second day.

Dessert Notes

PIES AND CRUSTS

NEVER FAIL PIE CRUST (2 - 9" CRUSTS)

SIFT 2 C FLOUR AND 1 TSP SALT. REMOVE 1/3 C AND MIX WITH 1/4 C WATER TO FORM A PASTE. CUT 2/3 C CRISCO INTO THE REMAINING FLOUR UNTIL IT'S LIKE COARSE MEAL. ADD THE PASTE AND MIX UNTIL IT ALL CLINGS TOGETHER. DIVIDE IN HALF AND FORM INTO BALLS. ROLL OUT ON A FLOURED BOARD.

ADVENTURE CRUST (2 - 9" CRUSTS)

2 1/2 C FLOUR   1 TSP. SALT   1/2 C MILK
2/3 C LARD   1 1/2 TBLSP. VINEGAR

SOUR THE MILK WITH VINEGAR. MIX FLOUR AND SALT AND CUT THE LARD IN. ADD MILK TO FLOUR MIX ALL AT ONCE. FORM INTO A DOUGH, HANDLING GENTLY. ROLL OUT.

There's an infinite variety of crumb crusts to be made using different types of cookies or cereals. The graham cracker crust is the most widely used. Now, why not try one of the following for a change.

KIND	BUTTER	CRUMBS	SUGAR
16-18 GRAHAM CRACKERS	1/3 C	1 1/3 C	1/4 C
16 CHOCOLATE OREOS	1/4 C	1 1/3 C	0
19 CHOCOLATE WAFERS	1/4 C	1 1/3 C	0
24 VANILLA WAFERS	1/4 C	1 1/3 C	0
18 SHORTBREAD COOKIES	2 TBLSP.	1 1/4 C	0
14 OATMEAL COOKIES	1/4 C	1 1/4 C	0
20 GINGERSNAPS	1/3 C	1 1/3 C	0
14 CHOCOLATE CHIP COOKIES	2 TBLSP.	1 1/4 C	0
CEREAL FLAKES	1/4 C	1 1/3 C	2 TBLSP.
ROLLED OATS	1/3 C	1 1/4 C	1/3 C BROWN

Crush cookies or cereal between waxed paper. Mix in sugar and work in soft butter with a fork. Press into a pie tin (you may set aside a couple of tblsp. for topping, depending on the filling). With any of them, you can reduce the crumbs to 1 C and add ½ C finely chopped walnuts, pecans, almonds or brazil nuts. With oatmeal, add a couple tblsp. of wheat germ. Other additions that are interesting to a crust: 1 tblsp poppy or sesame seed, 1 tsp. grated citrus rind or reduce crumbs ¼ C and add coconut.

APPLE PIE

Line pie pan with pastry. Mix together ⅔ C white or brown sugar, ⅛ tsp. salt, 2 tblsp. flour (or 1½ tblsp. cornstarch). Toss gently with six C sliced tart apples. Place in layers in shell. Dot with 1½ tblsp. butter and sprinkle with 1 tblsp. lemon juice. Cover with top crust or <u>STREUSEL TOPPING</u>: ½ C light brown sugar, ¼ C butter, ⅓ C flour and ¼ tsp. cinnamon. Mix with fingers to consistency of coarse crumbs. Pat on top of apples. Bake at 450° for ten minutes, then at 350° for about 40 minutes. If using regular crust, brush with milk before baking.

BLUEBERRY PIE

Line pie pan with pastry. Combine 3 tblsp. quick-cooking tapioca with ⅔ C sugar. Blend gently with one quart of blueberries. Let stand fifteen minutes, then season with 1½ tblsp. lemon juice and ½ tsp. cinnamon (optional). Fill pie shell with berries, dot with butter and cover with the top crust. Bake at 450° for ten minutes and then at 350° for 40 minutes.

Sometimes we'll use combinations of fruits in a pie. Blueberry-peach is a favorite. Peach pie is nice if flavored with almond. Peach pie takes less sugar than apple. Rhubarb pie needs more. — To 4 c rhubarb, use 1/4 c flour and 1 1/2 – 2 c sugar, 1 tblsp. butter, and grated orange rind.

PUMPKIN PIE

1 1/4 c pumpkin   1/2 tsp. nutmeg   3/4 c evaporated milk
1 c brown sugar   1/2 tsp. salt   2 tblsp. molasses
1 tblsp. flour   3 beaten eggs   9" unbaked pie shell
1 tsp. ginger   grates of 1 orange   8 walnut halves
1/2 tsp. cinnamon   1/2 c orange juice

Combine pumpkin, sugar, flour, spices, salt, eggs, rind, juice, molasses and milk. Pour into shell. Float walnuts on top. Bake at 450° for 15 minutes. Reduce heat to 350° and bake 30 minutes more, or until firm.

Cottage Cheese Pie

2 c cottage cheese   juice of 2 oranges
rind 1 lemon   3 eggs, beaten
juice 1 lemon   1/4 tsp. salt   1 c sugar

Seive cottage cheese and add everything else. Mix and pour into a pastry-lined 9" pie pan. Bake at 450° for 10 minutes, then at 350° for 25 minutes until firm.

Pecan Pie

Beat 3 eggs very light. Slowly beat in 3/4 c sugar, 1/4 c melted butter, 1 c brown corn syrup, 1/2 tsp. salt and 1 tsp. vanilla. Stir in 1 c broken pecans and pour into a pie shell that has been pre-baked at 450° for five minutes. Bake at 375° for 40 minutes until firm.

QUICK CUSTARD PIE

2 C MILK	4 EGGS	1 1/2 TSP. VANILLA
1/2 C SUGAR	1/4 C BUTTER	1/2 C BISQUICK

BEAT ALL TOGETHER AND POUR INTO A GREASED, FLOURED 9" PIE PAN. BAKE AT 375° UNTIL SET ~ 30-40 MINUTES. SPRINKLE NUTMEG ON TOP. CUSTARD WILL RISE AND A CRUST FORM ON THE BOTTOM. TO VARY, ADD COCONUT OR NUTS.

LEMON CURD PIE

4 LARGE EGGS	1/4 C SOFT BUTTER
1/8 TSP. SALT	2 TBLSP. GRATED LEMON PEEL
1 3/4 C SUGAR	1/2 C LEMON JUICE

BEAT EGGS IN THE TOP OF A DOUBLE BOILER. STIR IN SALT, SUGAR, BUTTER, LEMON PEEL AND JUICE. COOK OVER HOT WATER ABOUT 30 MINUTES, STIRRING FREQUENTLY, UNTIL THICK AND SMOOTH. WHEN COOL, FOLD IN 1 C WHIPPED CREAM OR COOL WHIP AND PILE IN COOKED PIE CRUST. OR PUT IN SHELL AS IS AND TOP WITH SOUR CREAM OR WHIPPED CREAM.

JAN'S CREAM PIE

1/2 C SUGAR	2 C MILK	1 TSP. VANILLA
4 TBLSP. FLOUR	2 EGG YOLKS, BEATEN	1-9" BAKED PIE SHELL
1/4 TSP. SALT	2 TBLSP. BUTTER	

MIX DRY INGREDIENTS IN TOP OF DOUBLE BOILER WITH 1/2 C MILK. ADD REMAINING MILK. COOK OVER BOILING WATER, STIRRING, UNTIL THICK. COVER AND COOK 15 MINUTES LONGER, STIRRING OCCASIONALLY. ADD A COUPLE OF TBLSP. OF HOT MIX TO EGG YOLKS. STIR AND COMBINE WITH THE FILLING IN THE POT. COOK 2 MINUTES LONGER. REMOVE FROM HEAT AND ADD BUTTER AND VANILLA. COOL SLIGHTLY. POUR INTO BAKED SHELL AND COVER WITH MERINGUE. BAKE AT 325° UNTIL MERINGUE IS LIGHTLY BROWNED.

MERINGUE - BEAT 2 EGG WHITES UNTIL FOAMY. ADD ¼ TSP. SALT AND 4 TBLSP. SUGAR AND BEAT UNTIL GLOSSY AND STIFF PEAKS FORM.

    COCONUT PIE - ADD ½ C SHREDDED COCONUT TO THE CREAM FILLING. SPRINKLE MERINGUE WITH COCONUT BEFORE BROWNING.

NOTES

Recipe INDEX

APPETIZERS

CLAM DIP	44
CLAM POT	44
CRAB DIP	44
HAM DIP OR SPREAD	43
LOBSTER DIP	44
PICKLED FISH	45
RED-HOT DIP	43
SEVICHE	45
SHRIMP DIP	43
SPINACH DIP	42
SUNSHINE DIP	43
VEGETABLE DIP #1	42
VEGETABLE DIP #2	42

BREADS

ANADAMA BREAD	57
BANANA BREAD, MOIST	52
BANANA BREAD, BRAN	51
BASIC BREAD, YEAST	55
BISCUITS, BAKING PWD.	47
BROWN BREAD, STEAMED	61
BUTTERMILK CHEESE BREAD	56
CINNAMON ROLLS	55
COFFEECAKE, BUTTERMILK	51
COFFEECAKE, QUICK	50
CORN BREAD	49

CORNMEAL BRAID	56
CRANBERRY NUT BREAD	53
DATE NUT BREAD	52
DATE NUT BREAD, YEAST	61
GRANOLA CEREAL	62
IRISH SODA BREAD	54
MUFFINS	48
BLUEBERRY	48
BRAN	48
OATMEAL	49
NEWFOUNDLAND BREAD	57
OATCAKES, SCOTCH	50
OATMEAL RAISIN BREAD	53
OATMEAL BREAD, YEAST	58
OATMEAL BREAD, YEAST, (COOKED)	58
PANCAKES	PP. 46-47
BUCKWHEAT CAKES	46
CORN GRIDDLE CAKES	46
OATMEAL PANCAKES	47
SOUR MILK PANCAKES	46
PUMPKIN BREAD	54
PUMPKIN RAISIN ROLLS	60
RAISIN BREAD	61
RYE BREAD, OLD WORLD	60
SPOONBREAD, CHEDDAR	50
SPROUTED WHEAT BREAD	59
WHEAT GERM BREAD	59
WHEAT ORANGE BREAD	53
ZUCCHINI BREAD	52
YORKSHIRE PUDDING	84

EGG DISHES

BUCKEYE BRUNCH	66
CREAMED EGGS	65
MUSHROOM POACH	65
QUICHE	67
RED EYE POACH	65
SAUSAGE BUCK	66
SCRAMBLED EGGS	64

SANDWICHES

CHICKEN OR TURKEY SALAD FILLING	68
EGG SALAD SANDWICH FILLING	68
HAM SALAD FILLING	68
SEASONED TOAST	69
TUNA SALAD FILLING	69

STUFFINGS

CORN BREAD	70
FISH, STUFFING FOR	71
FRUIT STUFFING	71
PINEAPPLE STUFFING	71
RICE STUFFING	70
TRADITIONAL	70

SOUPS AND CHOWDERS

CLAM CHOWDER	72
CORN CHOWDER	73
FISH CHOWDER	72
LENTIL SOUP	74
LOBSTER BISQUE	73
MINESTRONE	75
PEA SOUP	74

Pumpkin Soup	75
Tomato Bisque	74

LUNCHEON HOT DISHES

Chicken or Turkey Loaf	79
Chile	76
Ham Loaf	79
Fog Chaser	76
Meat Loaf	79
Pizza	78
Red Flannel Hash	78
Spaghetti Sauce	77
Stir Fried Rice	77

SALADS

Green Salad	82
Lime-Cheese Mold	83
Orange-Onion	83
Potato Salad	81
Rice Salad	81
Rice and Bean Salad	81
Roast Beef Salad	82
Slaw, Pineapple	80
Slaw, Tangy	80
Spinach Salad, Wilted	80

SALAD DRESSINGS

Fruit, Dressing for	83
Garlic Dressing	82
Tomato French	82

MEAT, FOWL AND FISH

BEEF	84
CHICKEN, COUNTRY	87
CHICKEN, OVEN FRIED	86
CHICKEN, MANDARIN	87
CHICKEN, SHERRIED	86
CORNED BEEF	88
FISH, "AH SO"	85
FISH, BAKED HADDOCK	84
FISH, FLORENTINE	85
FISH, MACADAMIA	85
FISH, OVEN FRIED	86
FISH, STUFFED	86
HAM	87
LAMB	84
NEW ENGLAND BOILED DINNER	89
TURKEY, PORK	84

MEAT SAUCES

FRUIT COMPOTE	88
HORSERADISH SAUCE	88
RAISIN SAUCE	88

VEGETABLES

ARTICHOKE CASSEROLE	90
BEANS, GREEN	90
BEANS, SWEET AND SOUR	90
BEANS, BAKED	91
BEETS	91
BEETS, HARVARD	91
BEETS AND SOUR CREAM	91
BROCCOLI	92

BRUSSELS SPROUTS	92
CABBAGE, BRAISED	92
CABBAGE IN MUSTARD SAUCE	92
CABBAGE, RED	93
CARROTS, CRAZY	93
CARROTS, GINGER	93
CARROTS, STIR-FRIED	93
CAULIFLOWER, CHINESE	94
CAULIFLOWER, PAPRIKA	94
CAULIFLOWER, SESAME	94
CORN, FRESH CREAMY	95
CORN OYSTERS	96
CORN PUDDING	95
CORN RELISH	95
CORN, TOMATO AND PEPPER CASSEROLE	96
CORN, VEGETABLE CASSEROLE	96
EGGPLANT, EASY EASTERN	97
EGGPLANT, DEEP FRIED	97
EGGPLANT, MIDDLE EAST	97
EGGPLANT, SKILLET PARMESAN	97
NOODLES, SOUR CREAM	98
ONIONS AND APPLE CASSEROLE	99
ONIONS, BAKED STUFFED	99
ONION PIE	99
ONIONS, PAPRIKA	98
ONIONS, SCALLOPED WITH PEANUTS	98
PEAS	100
POTATO PANCAKES	100
POTATOES, SCALLOPED	101
POTATO SOUFFLÉ	100
POTATOES, SWEET, BRANDIED	101

POTATOES, SWEET, PUFFED	101
POTATOES, SWEET, SWEET AND SOUR	102
RICE, APPLE	103
RICE, CURRIED RAISIN	103
RICE, HERB	102
RICE, MUSHROOM	102
RICE, NUT	102
RICE AND PEAS	102
RICE PILAF	103
RICE SOUFFLÉ	104
RICE, SPANISH	103
SPINACH INTRIGUE	105
SPINACH MOLD	104
SPINACH, STUFFED	105
SPINACH TART	105
SQUASH, BAKED	106
SQUASH, FRENCH FRIED ZUCCHINI	106
SQUASH, ZUCCHINI, FRITATA	107
SQUASH, GREEN AND GOLD	106
SQUASH, ZUCCHINI LOAF	107
SQUASH, SCALLOPED	107
SQUASH, SUMMER	106
SQUASH, WINTER	106
SQUASH, ZUCCHINI – TOMATO LAYERS	107
TOMATO – CHEESE CUSTARD	108
TOMATO QUICHE	109
TOMATO OYSTERS	109
TOMATO PUDDING	109
TOMATOES, SCALLOPED	108
TOMATO STUFFING	108

VEGETABLE SAUCES

Hollandaise	92
Jiffy Hollandaise	92

CAKES

Almond Cake	113
Applecake	114
Applesauce Spice	114
Blueberry Pudding Cake	114
Carrot Nut Cake	115
Cheesecake	128
Cheesecake, Pumpkin	129
Chocolate Cake	116
Fruit Cocktail Cake	115
Gingerbread	115
Hundred Dollar Cake	111
Marlin Spike Cake	111
Pineapple Upside Down Cake	113
Pound Cake	112
Shortcake	47
Sponge Cake, Hot Milk	112

FROSTINGS

Boiled White	112
Chocolate	116

DESSERT SAUCES

Butterscotch	127
Chocolate #1	127
Chocolate #2	127
Lemon, Quick	116
Pudding or Cake Sauce	116

COOKIES

BROWNIES	120
BUTTERSCOTCH FRUIT BARS	120
CARAMEL BROWNIES	120
CHOCOLATE, MOM'S	121
CINNAMON CRUNCH	118
GRANOLA COOKIES	119
MOLASSES COOKIES	119
OATMEAL COOKIES	119
PEANUT BUTTER	119
SEVEN LAYER BARS	120
SCOTCH SHORTBREAD	118
SWEDISH SPICE	118

DESSERTS, MISCELLANEOUS

APPLESAUCE PUDDING	124
BREAD PUDDING	123
BUTTERSCOTCH PUDDING	122
CHERRY SOG	125
CHOCOLATE PUDDING	122
COBBLER	125
COFFEE SOUFFLÉ	126
CRAZY PUDDING	123
CRUNCH PUFF PUDDING	124
FRUIT CRISP	125
ICE CREAM	128
INDIAN PUDDING	127
LEMON SOUFFLÉ	124
RICE CREAM	126
RICE PUDDING	126
VANILLA PUDDING	122
YOGURT	128

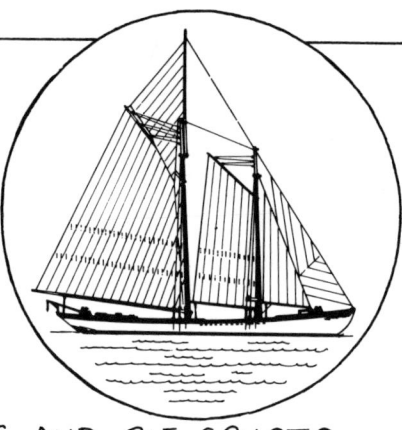

PIES AND PIE CRUSTS

ADVENTURE CRUST	130
APPLE PIE	131
BLUEBERRY PIE	131
CEREAL FLAKE CRUST	130
CHOCOLATE CHIP COOKIE CRUST	130
CHOCOLATE OREO CRUST	130
CHOCOLATE WAFER CRUST	130
COTTAGE CHEESE PIE	132
CREAM PIE, JAN'S	133
CUSTARD PIE, QUICK	133
GINGERSNAP CRUST	130
GRAHAM CRUST	130
LEMON CURD PIE	133
NEVER FAIL CRUST	130
OATMEAL COOKIE CRUST	130
PECAN PIE	132
PUMPKIN PIE	132
ROLLED OATMEAL CRUST	130
SHORTBREAD COOKIE CRUST	130
VANILLA WAFER CRUST	130

A WINDJAMMER SAMPLER

THUMBNAIL SKETCHES OF SOME VESSELS THAT WORK OR HAVE WORKED IN THE NEW ENGLAND WINDJAMMER FLEET.

★ How Windjamming Vacations Began

In the 1930's, Frank Swift was involved with a boys' camp in Maine. Although his background was in silversmithing and painting, he had been a cadet on a merchant marine barkentine and had voyaged to the Orient as crew on a Barber Line freighter. He was enamoured of the Maine coast and its working coastal schooners.

He arranged for the campers and counselors to sail on a schooner for a week and subsequently decided it would be a wonderful trip for anyone. From 1936 and 25 years thereafter, he acquired vessels — sometimes chartering and then buying them. He converted cargo or fishing vessels into "dude cruisers" to carry passengers during the summer months, thus extending the useful life of many of these ships, creating a tradition that's still going strong today.

STEPHEN TABER

68-FT. SCHOONER
22 PASSENGERS
6 CREW

Built in 1871 in Glenwood Landing, N.Y. (Long Island Sound). Known as the oldest documented U.S. sailing vessel in continuous service. She carried bricks and cement on the Hudson River. Brought to Maine in the 20's, she was completely rebuilt in the 1930's and used in the pulpwood business along the Maine coast.

She entered the passenger business in 1946 under Captain Frederick B. Guild. She has started several skippers in the Maine windjammer trade — including Cy Cousins, Havilah Hawkins, Jim Sharp, Orvil Young, Mike Anderson, Ken Barnes.

She's known as a good luck ship, and a happy one.

She was rebuilt in the winter of 1981/82 at the North End Shipyard in Rockland under Captain Ken Barnes.

TIMBERWIND

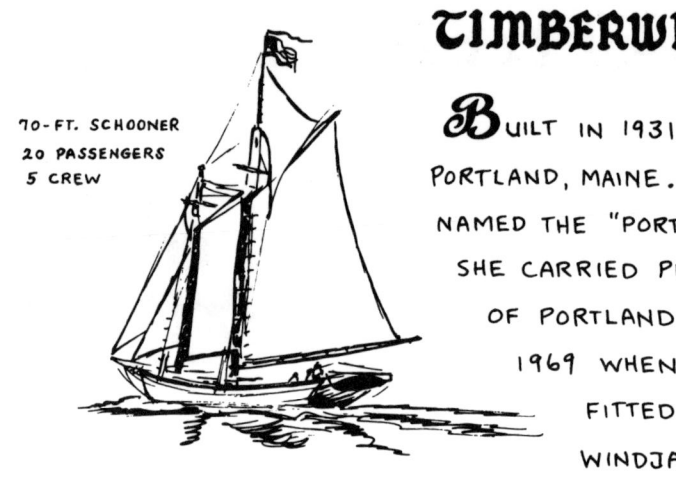

70-FT. SCHOONER
20 PASSENGERS
5 CREW

Built in 1931 in Portland, Maine. Originally named the "Portland Pilot", she carried pilots out of Portland until 1969 when she was fitted out for windjammer work.

HARVEY GAMAGE

Built in 1973 at South Bristol, Maine in the Harvey Gamage shipyard especially for carrying passengers under sail. Works on the Maine coast in the summer months and in the fall, sails to the Caribbean to make winter cruises.

95-FT. SCHOONER
32 PASSENGERS
5 CREW

LEWIS R. FRENCH

Built in 1871 in Christmas Cove (near South Bristol, Maine). The "French" was a coaster.* She and the "Stephen Taber" are the oldest schooners on the bay. Carried freight and codfish along the coast. Converted to power in the 20's, she then hauled fish for sardine factories. She was restored to her original schooner rig at the North End Shipyard in Rockland, Maine and joined the fleet in 1976.

64 FT. SCHOONER
22 PASSENGERS
4 CREW

The "Lewis R. French" is the only survivor of all the coastal schooners built in Maine in the nineteenth century.

---

* Coasters were sailing craft carrying cargoes from one coastal port to another — not considered deep-water vessels, their hey-day was the mid 1800's until World War I, before good roads were built.

MARY DAY

83-FT. SCHOONER
28 PASSENGERS
6 CREW

Built in 1962 in South Bristol, Maine, specifically to carry passengers by Captain Havilah Hawkins. She was the first of her type (a centerboard schooner) to be built in thirty years for commercial use and the first constructed for the sole purpose of carrying passengers under sail.

NATHANIEL BOWDITCH

Built in 1922 in East Boothbay, Maine as a racing yacht, she participated in Newport to Bermuda races. During World War II she was used by the Coast Guard as a coastal patrol boat. In 1971 she was rebuilt for the passenger trade, and her name was changed to "Nathaniel Bowditch", in honor of the 18th century mathematician.

81-FT. SCHOONER
22 PASSENGERS
5 CREW

ISAAC H. EVANS

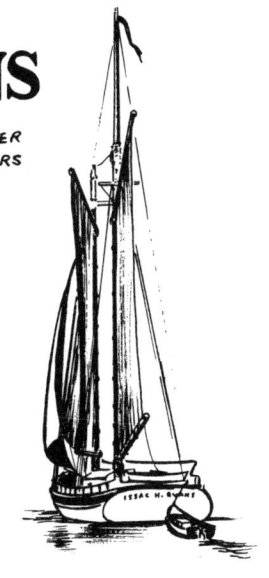

BUILT IN 1886

64-FT. SCHOONER
22 PASSENGERS
4 CREW

IN MAURICETOWN, NEW JERSEY. SHE SPENT 85 YEARS FREIGHTING AND OYSTERING ON DELAWARE BAY. HER ORIGINAL NAME WAS "BOYD N. SHEPHERD". IN 1971 SHE WAS REBUILT AT THE PERCY AND SMALL SHIPYARD, BATH, MAINE. SHE FIRST SAILED WITH THE WINDJAMMER FLEET IN 1973.

ANGELIQUE

95-FT. KETCH
31 PASSENGERS
7 CREW

BUILT IN 1980 IN PALATKA, FLORIDA. SHE HAS A STEEL HULL WITH WATERTIGHT COMPARTMENTS AND 2 DIESEL ENGINES. BUILT BY MIKE ANDERSON FOR THE TRADE. WITH HER PLUMB BOW AND GAFF KETCH RIG, SHE RESEMBLES ENGLISH TRAWLERS BUILT AT THE TURN OF THE CENTURY.

J. & E. RIGGIN

89-FT. SCHOONER
26 PASSENGERS
5 CREW

Built in 1927 in Dorchester, New Jersey. A centerboarder, she dredged oysters on Delaware Bay. Captain Dave and Sue Allen spent two years restoring her at the North End Shipyard in Rockland and put her into passenger service in 1977.

VICTORY CHIMES

Built in 1900 in Bethel, Delaware as the "Edwin and Maud". Her type is known as a centerboard "ram". She carried lumber and freight on the Chesapeake and along the coast from the Carolinas to New York.

First sailed in the 1950's with passengers on the Maine coast under Captain Frederick Guild. The "Chimes" was retired in 1987 from the New England passenger trade.

132-FT. SCHOONER
44 PASSENGERS
11 CREW

ROSEWAY

112-FT. SCHOONER
37 PASSENGERS
7 CREW

Built in 1925 at Essex, Mass. She was used as a yacht, and spent some time in the sport of swordfishing. In 1941 the Boston Pilots bought her and she served as a pilot boat into the 1970's. She has an auxiliary engine and watertight bulkheads. She began sailing passengers out of Camden in 1975 under Captain Orvil Young.

MERCANTILE

80-FT. SCHOONER
26 PASSENGERS
5 CREW

Built in 1916 on Little Deer Isle, Maine. Served as a freighter among the islands of Maine, carrying pulpwood to lime kilns in Rockland and Rockport. She joined Captain Frank Swift's fleet of windjammers in 1942. Swift eventually operated a dozen such vessels.

Adventure

120-FT. SCHOONER
37 PASSENGERS
7 CREW

Built in 1926 in Essex, Mass. A Gloucester dory fishing "knockabout",* she fished until 1954 and was the all time "high liner".**

She has a sleek hull to speed the haddock (in the winter) and halibut (in the summer) from the Grand Banks to market in Gloucester. She was put into the passenger sailing business in the 1960's and run by Captain Jim Sharp from 1965 until her retirement in 1987.

* Knockabout - without a bowsprit.

** High Liner - "Adventure" is credited with having caught and carried to market more pounds of fish than any other vessel sailing out of Gloucester.

HERITAGE

94-FT. SCHOONER
34 PASSENGERS
6 CREW

Built in 1983 in Rockland, Maine. Designed along the lines of a nineteenth century coaster and built by Captains Doug and Linda Lee at the North End Shipyard. The first vessel of this type to be launched in over 60 years.

AMERICAN EAGLE
85-FT. SCHOONER

28 PASSENGERS
5 CREW

Built in 1930 in Gloucester, Mass. as the "Andrew and Rosalie", she worked as a fishing vessel (an eastern-rigged dragger- converted from the last of the Gloucester schooners) until 1983 when Captain John Foss brought her to the North End Shipyard in Rockland and restored her original sailing rig. She has an auxiliary engine and sailed her first season with passengers in 1986.

SYLVINA W. BEAL

78-FT. SCHOONER
18 PASSENGERS
4 CREW

*B*uilt in 1911 in East Boothbay, Maine. Construction - sawn oak frames, trunnel fastened and oak planked - hackmatack knees around the mast step. The last sailing sardine carrier built in Maine, she carried fish from vessels off the Isle of Shoals to packing houses on the mainland. When converted to power in the 30's, her rig was cut down. In 1980 Captain John Worth restored her schooner rig and she was set up to carry passengers.

MATTIE

80-FT. SCHOONER
29 PASSENGERS
5 CREW

*B*uilt in 1882 in Patchogue, N.Y. She sailed with the "Box Board"* fleet and in the late 1800's was in the West Indies fruit trade. She carried granite to New York City for the old Post Office Building and Grand Central Station. She began sailing passengers in the 1940's under Captain Swift.

* Boxboards were rough planks with the bark still intact. They had to be handled one at a time. It was hard on the hands and the uneven edges didn't stow as closely as finished lumber. Stacked fore and aft until the height of the rail and then alternately athwartships in layers, they extended several feet outboard.

BOWDOIN

88-FT. SCHOONER

Built in 1921 in East Boothbay, Maine. Drawn by the famous yacht designer William Hand. She was heavily constructed for Arctic exploration and made 26 voyages under Admiral Donald B. MacMillan. During World War II, she was used by the Navy as a pilot ship for Allied vessels entering Greenland.

In 1980 the "Bowdoin" underwent a complete restoration at the Percy and Small shipyard in Bath, Maine, and in 1983 began a new career as a seagoing school ship. She's recognized from a distance by the ice barrel on her fore spreader (enclosed crow's nest, for crew protection - used when aloft looking for ice).

Occasionally a windjammer is retired to pasture and from time to time a new one is added to the lists. But the good down east cooking remains a constant factor in this unique fleet.

For readers who develop a yearning to taste windjammer cooking first hand (and savor all the other experiences a windjammer cruise has to offer), a note to one of the sources below should bring details about schedules, costs, etc.:

    WINDJAMMER ASSOCIATION
    P. O. Box 317
    ROCKPORT, MAINE 04856

LOCAL CHAMBERS OF COMMERCE IN CAMDEN, ROCKPORT, ROCKLAND, BOOTHBAY HARBOR, OR PORTLAND, MAINE.
    OR
SCAN THE ADS IN THESE TWO NEW ENGLAND MAGAZINES —
   ① DOWNEAST MAGAZINE
     CAMDEN, MAINE 04843
   ② YANKEE MAGAZINE
     DUBLIN, N. H. 03444

The last of sixteen thousand ships*
　now sail upon the bay,
and carry summer visitors
　one half a world away.

The remnants of a schooner fleet,
　the skin boats are the last
to sail from happy summer ports
　into a golden past.

The cargo in each ample hold
　is dreams instead of lime,
or pulp, or shakes, or merchandise
　from some far distant time.

So raise the tops'l to the breeze,
　or summon up a gale,
and sail away to yesterday
　and the golden days of sail.

　　　　— JAMES RUSSELL WIGGINS

*16,000 schooners were sighted off Owls Head in 1876.

By the same author

Maverick Sea Fare
WINDJAMMING AND COOKING IN THE CARIBBEAN

The Conch Book
THE NATURAL HISTORY OF THE QUEEN CONCH, WITH RECIPES

AVAILABLE FROM
PEN AND INK PRESS
P.O. BOX 235
WICOMICO CHURCH, VA. 22579